Bridges Between US

BRIDGES BETWEEN US

A PATHWAY TO UNITY THROUGH FAITH, EMPATHY & MUTUAL UNDERSTANDING

KHORI SMITH

with Michele Reber

XULON ELITE

Xulon Press Elite
2301 Lucien Way #415
Maitland, FL 32751
407.339.4217
www.xulonpress.com

Paperback ISBN-13: 978-1-6628-5509-2
Hard Cover ISBN-13: 978-1-6628-5510-8
Ebook ISBN-13: 978-1-6628-5511-5

To my wife Christine, whose life reflects the love, grace, humility and sacrifice that bridge building takes…

Table of Contents

Foreword

In response to the death and aftermath of George Floyd, I felt called to respond, particularly as it played out in my local church body. While racial reconciliation was a subject I was already deeply passionate about and had researched and written about for my thesis in seminary, the environment that this tragic event sparked created a new openness to the conversation in churches and in our nation. The huge divide in understanding and frames of reference between different ethnic groups was thrown into sharp relief in the days after our nation's airwaves were flooded with cell phone video of a black man dying under the knee of a white police officer. In an attempt to help bridge the gap, I began to develop a curriculum for a multi-week class/discussion group with the elders of my church. The curriculum aimed to look closely at God's heart regarding the challenges we faced and help provide some context around the interracial tensions that were simmering below the surface in the nation and the church at large. Much of this book reflects my life's study and that curriculum in the hopes it can be used in other church bodies wrestling with the same issues and questions.

Overall, my brother or sister holding this text, I invite you to read what follows with an open heart and open mind. Consider reading along with a friend, a partner, or a small group, so that discussion springs forth and experiences can be shared. This book isn't here to condemn or judge you. The goal is to create a safe space in which to have a conversation; one I hope you'll continue long after finishing this book.

Introduction:

What's Going On?

In 1971, Marvin Gaye asked a question in a song he released on the heels of the Civil Rights movement. It was a simple, but powerful question that beckoned the conscience of our nation to do some soul-searching regarding the pain and strife that existed among its people. He simply asked: "What's Goin'On?"

When he penned these familiar lyrics, the United States was in a constant state of social and political turmoil. The Vietnam War, the fight for women's equality, racism, calls for police reform, and divisive politics created a constant surge of public tension. This environment inspired the soul-searching question that Marvin would ask to the world: "Tell me, what's going on?" This song and this question were so highly regarded that it would propel the album to the top of the charts. According to Rolling Stone Magazine, it is the greatest album of all time[1] and remains the highest-selling album in the history of Motown Records[2].

The question Marvin was asking was not merely a rhetorical one. After years of endless social conflict, it was a plea for our nation and its people to search for a real answer to its cyclical divisive issues. I believe Marvin's question is still as relevant today as it was when he first asked it. What IS going on?

Perhaps what he was really asking was this: Why do we as human beings stay stuck in perpetual cycles of frustration, anger, and division toward our fellow man? Why are the same groups of people continually at odds with one another? Why are our personal experiences so different when we live in the same country? Will we ever cease fighting and being at war with one another?

Why Can't We Just All Get Along?

Maybe you've asked yourself this very question, but you've never felt compelled to engage it or try to find out why, as it seems to not have anything to do with you and your everyday world. Or maybe you have questions about the racial tensions you are seeing more and more of on your TV, but you feel like the current societal climate is just too volatile, the environment too judgmental. You might worry you'll be labeled or "canceled" for asking or saying the wrong thing, so you've shut down and avoided it altogether. Perhaps you feel enough progress has been made and that we all just need to be patient and content with where things are, considering where they used to be. Or maybe you've grabbed the bull by the horns and have been highly engaged in the conversation about race in America, but have found very few spaces where people are moving toward one another with love, patience, and grace for each other. Regardless of your experience, this book is for all of you.

In the last few years, it seems like the topic of race relations in the U.S. has grown to a fever pitch. The media is searching for answers; politicians, pundits and even churches have begun to engage in this topic. But despite our best efforts, we seem to be getting nowhere. The conversation remains highly polarized and divided to the point where each of the different "sides" are often just preaching to their own choirs. No one seems to be moving toward one another, just further away. But what if we all could put aside what we thought we knew long enough to find true answers? What if we could each push the "pause" button on our political viewpoints long enough to find common ground? What if we could discover the true source of our discontent and find the answer to Marvin Gaye's question once and for all? Might we find that there is something more, something better for all of us?

A Better Way?

Much of our current social media, news reporting, books, films, and television shows only seems to further entrench and polarize each side in their current beliefs as opposed to actually trying to reach across the divide and find some shared understanding that helps us move forward as a people. There is a lot of name-calling going on: names like "racist" or "white supremacist" and "bleeding heart liberal" or "woke" and "social justice warrior". Using these terms and others like them as we attempt conversation on the topic of today's tension only serves to put one side or the other on the defense and makes assumptions that don't allow for each person's unique frame of reference and lived experience. As a result, maybe you've sat out this very conversation in fear of being judged, labeled, and made to feel like a villain while exploring the issue. Maybe you've tried to engage, but found that everyone seems afraid or triggered on this topic and already irreversibly dug into their own viewpoints.

This book strives to be different. It is for people like you, who want to understand more about what's happening in our world around the issues of color, race, culture, and the context we live in through a Biblical lens – *without* feeling attacked or judged from the very outset. Some of the information shared here might not be familiar to you, which is totally okay. We are all learning new things all the time! My hope is that what is shared here will help enhance your understanding of what's happening today while presenting a Biblical basis for how we as Christ-followers might show up in the race conversation with love and a heart to help heal this divide. My desire is to draw the various sides and viewpoints toward one another in a new conversation filled with grace and truth.

Don't worry, this book is NOT here to turn you into a Democrat, or a Republican, for that matter. It's not about politics or being "politically correct". It is about looking at these issues through the lens of faith and helping you, the reader, the one who dares to discover, understand more about the historical context influencing the different "sides" in our nation that perpetuate this divisive climate. The truth is, these cycles of division will never go away until we look at them honestly without our predetermined, immovable political ideological biases – all of which can prevent us from moving towards common ground.

What if truth and integrity didn't pick sides? What if it turns out that the truth is inconvenient for us all? What if it's not so much an "either/or" but actually more of a "both/and"? What if embracing the truth drew us toward one another in a new way instead of just driving us further apart? What if we built a conversation so honest that it required us to move toward one another to engage in it?

What do we have to lose by listening to a different viewpoint or trying to understand the lived experience of someone who doesn't share our skin color? It can be extremely triggering when our political and theological beliefs – our worldview, essentially – are challenged. But often when we allow ourselves to be curious about *why* we are so triggered, we create an opportunity for self-growth. Often when we feel our beliefs being challenged or threatened, and we get angry or shut down, it can be an indication that, on some level, we are aware something is not quite right in *ourselves.*

As we begin this journey, it's important to know that it will not be the easiest one we've ever been on; bridge-building never is. Bringing two sides together is hard work – it takes incredible sacrifice and resources to close the divide. But the benefits of bridge-building are always exponential.

Bridging the Gap

China has been building bridges for centuries. Throughout the country's history, the bridges they've built have yielded exceptional results. When China set out to build the Sidu River Bridge, everyone knew the endeavor would be hard, dangerous, and *costly.* This bridge was designed to span three-quarters of a mile across a cavernous, dangerous ravine, suspended 1,627 feet into the sky! Can you imagine being one of the brave men or women who had to work on this bridge while it was still being completed? The chasm was so wide that they had to fire rockets from one side to the other just to begin the project and lay its foundation. To top it off, the project would cost a staggering 720 million yuan (approximately US $100 million)[3].

But it was worthy of the cost. This bridge connected two major counties in a region that had never been joined in recorded history–bringing together people, organizations, and possibilities never before seen. Despite the very real obstacles, dangers, fears, and concerns, the project went forward because the benefit of completion would be a new reality that would create a better quality of life for everyone.

Sidu River Bridge. (Glabb)

That's what bridges do: they bridge the divide in an effort to help humanity overcome cavernous barriers and obstacles, creating new possibilities never seen before. Just think of how the bridges in your own town facilitate efficiency and ease in your daily life.

But in order to achieve this connectivity, we have to be willing to wade into the unknown and endure some mutual discomfort so we can reach one another on our opposing sides. This is especially true when we're looking to bridge the gap between different belief systems, life experiences, and perspectives. Emotions like anger, fear, anxiety, sadness, and hurt are bound to come up when we intentionally engage with viewpoints that differ from our own. However, when we persevere, those emotions eventually dissipate and we find a new balance and a more well-rounded outlook, if we're willing to be open to it.

That's what we are attempting to do in this discussion. I believe that spiritually and relationally, we are called to do the same thing. We are crossing the dividing chasm that few have dared to attempt to cross. I believe that as Christ-followers, if we are to reach others for Christ, and show the rest of the world we are Christians by our love, doing this uncomfortable work is the very thing Jesus calls us to do. In fact, this is one of the key things Jesus did in his ministry. He bridged a divide.

This passage from Ephesians following the Apostle Paul's words on the division between the Jews and the Gentiles of the day illustrates this very thing:

Ephesians 2:14-19 (NIV)

[14] *"For he himself is our peace, who has made the two groups one and has destroyed the barrier, the dividing wall of hostility,* [15] *by setting aside in his flesh the law with its commands and regulations. His purpose was to create in himself one new humanity out of the two, thus making peace,* [16] *and in one body to reconcile both of them to God through the cross, by which he put to death their hostility.* [17] *He came and preached peace to you who were far away and peace to those who were near.* [18] *For through him we both have access to the Father by one Spirit.* [19] *Consequently, you are no longer foreigners and strangers, but fellow citizens with God's people and also members of his household,"*

He himself is our peace. He has reconciled and made the two groups one. Jesus is the bridge that allowed peace between divided groups. In this passage, Paul is writing to the Ephesian church, a diverse church planted in a major Roman vacation city, visited by travelers from around the world. The church that was planted there reflected the diversity of cultures and ethnicities found in Ephesus, but as the early Christians with different backgrounds came together there, infighting and division started to occur. Tensions rose from historical rifts between certain people groups.

Jews weren't crazy about the Gentiles, Gentiles weren't crazy about the Jews, and nobody liked the Romans, all because of their cultural history.

Yet, according to the Bible, something radical occurred. Jesus brought peace between these groups and the groups actually became one. The cross did that. In Christ, peace is possible between groups.

In the Bible, we read story after story of how Christ brings unity, so why do we often find ourselves in this place of chronic division? What is preventing us as Christ-followers from pursuing our calling to work towards making His example a relational reality? These are the questions that we will explore.

Why So Black and White?

When it comes to working towards unity or talking about culture issues why does it seem like the dialogue always drifts heavily towards black and white culture issues? There is so much division in our world and other ethnic groups have unity issues too. What about God's heart for all people? This question often comes up in conversations regarding this topic and it's a good question. There are a <u>ton</u> of issues that divide people groups today, so you might ask why this book is focusing heavily on the division between Caucasians and African Americans. Even in our churches, it can sometimes seem that the primary focus is on these two people groups when engaging in conversations with the desire to increase oneness and unity within our congregations.

But what about the unique challenges Asian Americans face in this country? Latinos? Native Americans? These people groups all face hostility, stereotyping, and suffer from hate crimes. Unfortunately, one book cannot realistically address all of the ethnic and cultural challenges in our country or world. Additionally, one of the major obstacles to experiencing the kind of oneness that God desires to see exist in His creation, and specifically in the Church body in America, is the historical context and underlying tension between African Americans and Caucasians. Here in the U.S., the relationship between African Americans and Caucasians has always seemed to be the place with the greatest amount of tension. It's where our national wound seems to keep opening up, never fully healing. If you turn on the TV and watch the news, this is the primary place of tension in our country and so this book's focus will be on this conversation. That being said, there will be a ton of relevant insights that will help you engage in conversations about racial and ethnic tensions regarding other people groups as well.

Overall, dear reader, you are invited to read what follows with an open heart and open mind. This book isn't here to condemn or judge you...the goal is to create a safe space in which to have a conversation you'll continue long after finishing this book.

Questions for Reflection

1. What did Christ do on the cross for those once divided?

   Obsolve everyone as one

2. How might Christ's sacrifice impact the way we live our lives?

   Befriend everyone as one

3. What do physical bridges and relational bridges have in common?

   Predjudice, judgement

Chapter 1

Diversity vs. Oneness

There is a lot of talk today in various circles about the need for and benefit of diversity. Starbucks wants diversity, McDonald's wants diversity, colleges want diversity, and more recently, religious institutions of many different faiths have placed a new emphasis on diversity. Have you noticed?

The truth is, conversations surrounding diversity are often riddled with confusion, because everyone's idea of diversity and purpose for pursuing it is often vastly different, undefined, and ever-changing. In recent years, many businesses and organizations have emphasized diversity while not actually understanding why it matters in the first place. As a result, efforts to diversify can come across as a knee-jerk (albeit well-intentioned) reaction in the context of a tense racial climate in our nation. For many constituents, consumers, and congregants, unclear motives can lead to confusion, and rushed implementation of "diversity measures" can appear more like slapping a quick band-aid on a gaping head wound than an actual step towards true racial reconciliation.

If God's heart is for true oneness among people of all colors, perhaps the pursuit of increasing diversity as the end goal is missing the mark. Think about it: America has had exponential growth in diversity over the past century. If diversity itself was the cure on its own, we shouldn't still be seeing the racial tensions that exist today, right?

To make matters worse, the Church in America today doesn't even reflect the diversity we see in our neighborhoods. Each of the local congregations gathering to worship each week remain largely homogeneous. In fact, Sunday mornings in churches are the largest gatherings we have in our nation that continue to exist that way, but would making them more diverse in themselves even fix the underlying issues?

Consider for a moment that most of us experience diversity all the time: mall shoppers are diverse, movie theater audiences are diverse, football stadiums full of fans are diverse, restaurant-goers are diverse. Most of us spend at least a portion of our daily lives among people who don't look like us, yet as a society we're still experiencing racial disharmony.

That's because despite the diversity in these various environments, there really is no deep relational connection between the people present. When the movie ends, when the game is over, when the meal is finished, all of these diverse groups of people go back to their homes, which, for the majority of us, are places where there isn't a ton of diversity. Hanging out in diverse spaces tells us nothing about the relational depth or connectivity of those present. Proximity doesn't tell us a thing about relational unity.

Let's be honest – most of the major cities in America are very diverse, but there have obviously been historical challenges around how diverse people relate to one another within those cities. Here we see again that proximity to one another does not equate to connection. This is why pursuing diversity as an end in itself can lead to disappointment, confusion, and no greater love for one another. Many churches have discovered this as they have pursued diversity in an honest effort to fix things, but relationally, beyond the Sunday service, congregations are living out the rest of the week in their own homogeneous circles.

 Rather than calling for increased diversity, this book proposes the pursuit of "oneness" as a better goal, because oneness moves us from just existing in the room together towards experiencing and valuing life lived together. As people of faith, it seems natural that the Church would be the leader in this.

Biblical oneness is what happens when we pursue Jesus Christ's purposes for us with our whole hearts. It's what happens when we follow Him and His words and commands. When we do this, a true oneness is the overflow, with diversity merely a by-product. Biblical oneness moves us towards God and towards one another.

We see the kind of relationship that transcends superficial diversity in the Book of Acts, when the Church first began. On the Day of Pentecost, Jews came from all over to celebrate a great feast, and on that day, the Church took shape, as we see in the Scripture passage below:

Acts 2:5-11 (NIV)

[5] *"Now there were staying in Jerusalem God-fearing Jews from every nation under heaven. [6] When they heard this sound, a crowd came together in bewilderment, because each one heard their own language being spoken. [7] Utterly amazed, they asked: "Aren't all these who are speaking Galileans? [8] Then how is it that each of us hears them*

in our native language? ⁹ Parthians, Medes and Elamites; residents of Mesopotamia, Judea and Cappadocia, Pontus and Asia, ¹⁰ Phrygia and Pamphylia, Egypt and the parts of Libya near Cyrene; visitors from Rome ¹¹ (both Jews and converts to Judaism); Cretans and Arabs—we hear them declaring the wonders of God in our own tongues!"

First, notice who was there: Jews from many nations and backgrounds. If you dig a little further, you'll find that they were from some pretty diverse places. Let's look at a few:

– **Parthians**, **Medes** and **Elamites** were from a region that includes part of what we know as Iran today

– **Mesopotamia** is a region that encompasses present-day Iraq, parts of Turkey, Syria, and parts of Iran

– **Cappadocia** and **Pontus** were located in the area now known as Turkey

– **Judea** is present-day Israel

– **Egypt, Libya** and **Cyrene** are all located in Africa

The Bible says that there were also visitors from **Rome** (i.e., present-day Europe)! Wow.

This was a diverse group, and the Bible points this out for a reason, but not necessarily for the reason you might think. It wasn't just to merely celebrate diversity, but to show *what happened* with this diverse group. Diversity wasn't the goal, or perhaps the story would have stopped there.

What's revealed next is where we see the real power. This diverse group moved forward and did something. They became something not just in words but in how they lived.

Acts 2:42- 47 (NIV)

[42] *"They devoted themselves to the apostles' teaching and to fellowship, to the breaking of bread and to prayer. [43] Everyone was filled with awe at the many wonders and signs performed by the apostles. [44] All the believers were together and had everything in common. [45] They sold property and possessions to give to anyone who had need. [46] Every day they continued to meet together in the temple courts. They broke bread in their homes and ate together with glad and sincere hearts, [47] praising God and enjoying the favor of all the people. And the Lord added to their number daily those who were being saved."*

These people did life together! They saw and treated one another as brothers and sisters. They loved one another, looked out for one another, and respected one another. They recognized that the Gospel had the power to overcome the historical divisions between them and their very different cultures. Yes, there was bad history between some of these groups, but here we see this history pale in the light of the Holy Spirit's power.

This is what oneness looks like: pursuing God and life in a way that draws diverse people together. As believers, we should be champions of oneness in cultivating deep meaningful relationships, not merely appearing to be diverse. When we pursue Christ wholeheartedly without walls in our hearts toward one another, diversity will invariably show up as a byproduct. Diversity isn't just about skin color – it's also about the many different ways we each bring our cultural uniqueness to the table in Christ.

What Unites Us? God's Promise to Abraham

Every Sunday afternoon in the Fall, there are some of the most tense displays of division ever broadcast on television. The best athletes in the world compete against one another, fighting for every single inch and every yard for gridiron glory. I'm talking about football.

It's man against man, brother versus brother, friend versus friend, family versus family, my team versus your team. It's us versus them, purple versus blue, red versus green, Ravens versus Steelers, Patriots versus Colts, division versus division. It can get ugly! But despite all this tension, once a year in February, something amazing happens – all of the division goes away. Suddenly, individual players from each of the different teams come together as one, donning a new team uniform. They begin to work, collaborate, and dream together; they even share a playbook and root for one another to succeed. They join forces and become one in what is called the Pro Bowl.

For some fans, it's a relatively meaningless game played every year, but for others, it serves an extremely important purpose: it creates a demonstration of NFL unity.

Ultimately every player in the organization is on one team – they are all part of the NFL. The Pro Bowl players happen to represent some of the best in the league. Baltimore Ravens players hang out with Pittsburgh Steelers, Dallas Cowboys hang out with NY Giants, and Minnesota Vikings hang out with Chicago Bears. It's a full display of oneness and unity.

ie NFL Pro Bowl vs team vs team

And people wonder how these players from different teams become one when they have been divided against one another all year long. The answer is simple: they have a new identity.

While the players still represent their home teams, for a brief period of time they shed their home team identity and join a new team, the NFL Pro Bowl team. They all unite under one new banner and this new banner becomes their primary identity.

We see a similar idea of diverse people's identities uniting with a sense of "oneness" years earlier through the promise God made to Abraham. Abraham was a follower of God who was from the land of Mesopotamia (a region that today is home to Iraq, Kuwait, Syria and Turkey). The word Mesopotamia is actually derived from two ancient Greek words "meso," and "potamos." These words come together as one to mean "between two rivers"…the two rivers in this case being the Tigris and Euphrates[4].

Abraham was a middle-eastern man from that region who loved God, and the Lord used him mightily at the very beginning of the story of our oneness in God as believers. You read that right: a middle-eastern man sits as one of the most influential people in all of the Bible.

Let this sink in some. Many of us have grown up with pictures of Abraham as a man of European descent with a long white beard, but given his middle-eastern heritage, chances are that's not an accurate depiction. Here is just one powerful example of how God loves, values, and utilizes people of all colors for His divine purposes.

God speaks to Abraham and tells him that He will use him in a special way to bring God's purposes to the world:

Genesis 17: 4-7 (NIV)

[4] *"As for me, this is my covenant with you: You will be the father of many nations.* [5] *No longer will you be called Abram[a]; your name will be Abraham, for I have made you a father of many nations.* [6] *I will make you very fruitful; I will make nations of you, and kings will come from you.* [7] *I will establish my covenant as an everlasting covenant between me and you and your descendants after you for the generations to come, to be your God and the God of your descendants after you."*

As the text shows, God tells Abraham that he would father many nations. People from different cultures, races and backgrounds would recognize him as their father, thus uniting them as one. This was a radical concept in a time where tribalism was the norm and most people were divided up into groups based on shared interests, goals, and cultures. Yet, if we as believers ultimately look back to the same person, Abraham, as a *father,* in a unique way, this actually makes us siblings! This new identity, all originating from Abraham, brings us together in a powerful way and we become family – different cultures now united on one team. Paul talks about our family tree in Galatians 3:8 when he writes:

[8] *"Scripture foresaw that God would justify the Gentiles by faith, and announced the gospel in advance to Abraham: "All nations will be blessed through you."*

Amazing to think about! We see again clearly that God has a heart for bringing humanity together under His banner. His plan was not for our different cultures to divide and separate us because in our faith, we have the same father. Our ultimate Father is God Almighty, but he uses Abraham as an earthly example of the shared humanity that we have in faith. Abraham, a middle-eastern man, is part of the root that unites us.

Scripture beautifully illustrates this time and again. God has purposefully created a colorful tapestry. We see God's heart beckoning us toward one another throughout all of the Scriptures, but we have to have eyes to see. In reading the first few sections of this book you may already be noticing a trend about this idea of "oneness".

The Jeep Wave

Have you ever purchased a new car and then, almost immediately, you started seeing the same model as yours all over the road? It's unlikely that there are suddenly more cars of your make and model on the road than before, but now it feels like you have new eyes that allow you to see them everywhere!

Owners of Jeeps understand this on a deeper level. As a new Jeep buyer signs the paperwork for their shiny new 4x4, they may not be aware of the new "secret handshake" of the society they've just become a part of: the Jeep wave. Unbeknownst to other drivers of the world, when two Jeeps pass one another on the road, the drivers wave to one another. In other words, Jeep owners now have eyes to see other Jeeps on the road, and are so acutely aware of other Jeeps on the road that the wave becomes automatic. It is a gesture to acknowledge the familial bond of Jeep ownership! In fact, Jeep owners say they can spot another Jeep from miles away.

The truth is, the Bible is overflowing with the picture of God's heart for all people and nations. And it's not just a little secondary concept that pops up here and there – it's on nearly every page waving at you, if you have eyes to see it. As you read your Bible, I want to challenge you to read closer and really look at the locations, stories, nations, people, and places in a fresh way. I'll get you started with just one clear example from a well-known story.

One day Jesus was asked "What must I do to inherit eternal life'? And Jesus replied, "Love God with all your heart and love your neighbor as yourself". Loving God is the first and most important part. We have to love Him and His Word more than anything else. This enables us to obey the second command, which calls us to love others as ourselves. Loving one another as you love yourself is at the very heart of Biblical oneness. Unfortunately, loving others can be hard to do.

In fact, Jesus' reply triggered the man who posed the original question and he immediately asked Jesus "Who is my neighbor?" The answer Jesus gives literally changed the generally accepted definition of the word "neighbor": He tells the story of the Good Samaritan. This is a story that takes place within the context of the significant cultural and racial divide that existed between Jews and Samaritans in order to demonstrate the shared humanity of the two people groups and the need to have love for one another. In this story a Jewish man is beaten within an inch of his life and left on the side of the road by thieves. As he lays there dying, several of his fellow countrymen pass him by and do not come to his aid. However, a Samaritan (an ethnic group that historically hated the Jews) passes by the injured man and reaches across the cultural divide to help him in his time of need. The Samaritan treats the Jewish man like a brother and helps to heal him. So we see that one of the most famous stories in the Bible is all about treating others who aren't like us with love, empathy, and dignity. In fact, Jesus ends this story in Luke 10:36-37 (NIV):

[36] *"Which of these three do you think was a neighbor to the man who fell into the hands of robbers?"*

[37] *The expert in the law replied, "The one who had mercy on him." Jesus told him, "Go and do likewise."*

Jesus tells us to go and do likewise. His desire is for us to cross the cultural divide and to see each other as neighbors and to embrace one another.

However, we may not see the application to the racial tension in existence today, maybe because we haven't remembered what kind of vehicle we are in: not a Jeep, but God's heart for oneness among humanity. Once we remember, we begin to notice God's vision for oneness everywhere. Take a look and see in another snapshot – this time from Revelation 7:

Revelation 7:9-10 (NIV)

[9] *"After this I looked, and there before me was a great multitude that no one could count, from every nation, tribe, people and language, standing before the throne and before the Lamb. They were wearing white robes and were holding palm branches in their hands.* [10] *And they cried out in a loud voice: "Salvation belongs to our God, who sits on the throne, and to the Lamb."*

Notice the diversity in the imagery of this Scripture with salvation as the unifying factor. Salvation belongs to our God and oneness and diversity are the overflow. *Salvation* brought together a diverse group. As one, the multitude declares, "this is *our* God" and that fact draws them together as one. They sang one song, in one voice, with many hearts coming together as one.

Let's look at one more powerful example, one that is so familiar it can be easy to miss its unifying significance.

When Jesus was in His last few hours of His earthly suffering, the Romans beat him and then forced him to carry a cross through town. This was a common practice among the Romans as a form of public punishment in order to discourage others from getting out of line with Rome. The cross or beam that Jesus was forced to carry would have been very heavy and difficult to bear especially having just been beaten as Jesus was. So as Jesus is struggling to carry the heavy beam through the city, the following scene unfolds:

Matthew 27: 27-32 (NIV)

[27] *"Then the governor's soldiers took Jesus into the Praetorium and gathered the whole company of soldiers around him.* [28] *They stripped him and put a scarlet robe on him,* [29] *and then twisted together a crown of thorns and set it on his head. They put a staff in his right hand. Then they knelt in front of him and mocked him. "Hail, king of the Jews!" they said.* [30] *They spit on him, and took the staff and struck him on the head again and again.* [31] *After they had mocked him, they took off the robe and put his own clothes on him. Then they led him away to crucify him.* [32] *As they were going out, they met a man from Cyrene, named Simon, and they forced him to carry the cross."*

Did you catch that at the end? Simon of Cyrene helps Jesus carry His cross! Cyrene was located in Africa; this was an

African man who stepped in and in a powerful moment walked alongside Jesus. An African man and a Jew walked side by side in a pivotal moment where the entire town could see.

It would be easy to overemphasize the significance of this fact, but let's not ignore it, either. This picture in the life of Jesus is included in the Bible for a reason. In one of the most difficult moments in Christ's earthly residence, it is clear that God vividly sees the significance of all people, regardless of background, race, or color. That significance is illustrated over and over throughout the Scriptures. Sometimes it's explicit, but it's often subtle in its presentation, and so sometimes we have to look closely in order to draw it out.

If you still have any doubt about God looking past our human divisions in His vision for oneness, consider Paul's words in Galatians 3:28 (NIV):

Oneness

²⁸ *"There is neither Jew nor Gentile, neither slave nor free, nor is there male and female, for you are all one in Christ Jesus."*

Regardless of the barriers we humans come up with to separate ourselves, God breaks them down with His power, love, and Spirit. It is in this context that we'll continue our conversation about the racial divisions we see happening in our country today.

The Human Factor – We Are All Image Bearers

God's vision for oneness in the Church is clear, but what about people who don't share our faith? One of the keys in moving authentically toward one another is understanding how God sees *all* people. He pursues not just people in the Church who call on His name as Lord, but all of his created children who may not know Him yet. Scripture shows us clearly how we as human beings are seen by God. We can thank God that He saw us as His children, even before we knew Him as the Father.

Genesis 1:27 (NIV)

[27] *"So God created mankind in his own image, in the image of God he created them; male and female he created them."*

Consider for a moment that every person is made in the image of God. Let this idea marinate in your brain: God made mankind in *His own image.* This means there is something about <u>every person</u> that is reflective of the very Creator of the universe. This includes people who are not of our faith background – it includes every human being that has ever existed.

That leads us to the question: How should we view and treat one another as a result?

The easy answer is that every person is worthy of our love, care, and respect, but unfortunately, we often tend to embrace each other as image bearers only when viewing ourselves, our friends, and people we like. It can be harder to remember that *every* person on this globe is made in His image, including the people we aren't crazy about; the people who aren't like us; the people from other neighborhoods and towns we don't live in with whom we seemingly have nothing in common. Nevertheless, these "others" are also a reflection of God's own image. He is pursuing them with His love. Likewise, we are called to do the same.

As believers, we know that our ability to fully mirror God's image only starts to take shape as we surrender our lives to Jesus Christ and walk in His purposes for our lives. But even outside of that surrender, the role of bearing God's image is part of every single person's identity, whether they know it or not. This means that every single person is equally worthy of dignity and respect, period. This is God's idea for us. With respect to our shared identity as "image-bearers", we truly are one race – one people – human beings made in the image of their Creator. God is our Father, and nothing pleases a Father more than seeing His children in unity. As a father myself, nothing grieves me more than seeing my children fighting and at odds with one another.

This passage from Acts highlights the universal nature of how God sees us and promotes familial bonds between all of His precious sons and daughters.

Acts 17:26-28 (NIV)

[26] *"From one man he made all the nations, that they should inhabit the whole earth; and he marked out their appointed times in history and the boundaries of their lands.* [27] *God did this so that they would seek him and perhaps reach out for him and find him, though he is not far from any one of us.* [28] *'For in him we live and move and have our being.' As some of your own poets have said, 'We are his offspring.'*

It is true that God's very good creation of humankind includes a tremendous amount of diversity in our colors, our features, our languages, our cultures, our gifts, and our talents. It's also true that His desire is not for us to peacefully exist in our silos of difference, but to pursue oneness and unity as members of the same family.

Questions for Reflection

1. What strikes you about the Biblical account of Simon of Cyrene? How much thought or conversation have you engaged in on this part of the passage before?

    A man not a Jew united w/ Jesus & helped bear His burden

2. Can you recall other examples of both diversity and oneness that you've found in your past readings of Scripture? If so, what are they? Discuss them.

3. How do these examples inspire or challenge you?

4. What does this theme tell us about God's heart for us?

    Accept all, reject none despite others deeds & actions & race & beliefs

5. What does the passage from Acts 17 tell us about how God views all people? *Same answer as #4*

6. What does this mean for how we view other people, even those of different beliefs? Cultures? Socio-economic statuses?

Chapter 2

Déjà Vu: We've Seen This Before

The Universal Nature of Our Broken Hearts

I t is said that King Solomon was one of the richest men to ever live on the Earth. A comparative analysis in terms of today's currency reveals that he had more money than Jeff Bezos and Bill Gates combined. In fact, economic estimates of the income he gained from his gold mines have valued his net wealth at approximately $2.2 trillion in today's dollars[5]. It's safe to say Solomon had deep pockets!

In constant pursuit of fulfillment and meaning in life, Solomon used his money for all kinds of human exploits. While he didn't build his own space agency and launch a rocket into the sky, he did spend years and years pursuing many exciting ventures and conquests. Towards the end of his life, after everything he'd seen, done, and amassed, he discovered something unexpected about life and humanity and wrote these words in Ecclesiastes 1:9 (NIV):

[9] *"What has been will be again, what has been done will be done again; there is nothing new under the sun."*

Nothing new. The same thing happens over and over again in every generation. After all Solomon's searching, he realized that there really was nothing that was truly *new*. He observed and wrote about repetition and the cyclical nature of the human experience. He was having an existential form of déjà vu.

When observing our world today, we see a similar cyclical pattern when it comes to the human heart and some of the ups and downs we have faced. At our best, humans have shown the capacity to come together and create great things for the collective good, pushing humanity as a whole forward. History is full of stories of the innovation, creativity, love, and empathy humans have demonstrated for one another. However, when at our worst, we are drawn to believe that maybe we are better than others and so we divide and before you know it, we are colonizing to our heart's content. We believe our "betterness" makes us more suitable to control other people groups.

This belief comes from a deep sense of self-preservation intersecting with an assumption of scarcity, or finite resources. We always want the best for "me and mine", don't we? Unfortunately, this often leads to viewing others – especially those who don't look like us or speak our language – as competition for supremacy in terms of access to resources.

Humanity tends to use the norms and standards of each person's culture to judge the norms and standards of other cultures and we often end up, even unconsciously, judging and viewing others as inferior, or at least less deserving. This pervasive pattern is called "ethnocentrism". At its heart, it says "My people group is better than yours" and seeks to force the acceptance of that idea onto others with or without their consent. Whether we like it or not, ethnocentrism is a part of our human brokenness. In its most destructive application, ethnocentrism can lead to disdain or dislike for others and become the root cause for division, conflict, and oppression, often depending on which group is the majority, or who has the best access to capital and other life-sustaining resources.

Ethnocentrism has existed throughout the fabric of the world's history, at different times and places across the globe. If we look closely, we get a sobering sense of déjà vu. This thought was pervasive among the Egyptians, the Babylonians, the Macedonians, the Romans, the Mongols, the Normans, various European countries, and more recently through the formation of what became the sprawling British Empire. This is nothing new, nor was it new back in Old Testament times!

In fact, we see this dynamic in the Bible in one of the most tragic, yet inspiring stories ever told: The Exodus. The Bible tells us that the Egyptians had enslaved the Jewish people for four hundred years. During this time, they were stripped of their freedom and dignity and forced into manual labor in a dual effort to control their burgeoning population and influence, and also to continue to build up the nation of Egypt. They were beaten and whipped ruthlessly and lived in awful conditions. This story highlights a clear demonstration of God's heart towards this kind of suffering and atrocity. The Lord raises up Moses and utilizes him and others as agents of freedom for the oppressed Jewish people: "Let my people go free!"

One of the most famous stories of the Bible is about an oppressed people that God sets free.

We celebrate and love this biblical story; movies have been made about it. Yet, this story offers an early glimpse of ethnocentrism in all its ugliness. The general theme is sadly not uncommon. It reminds us that this pattern of one people group claiming superiority over another people group has been happening for a long time, and it continues to this day.

Consider for a moment the caste system in India. When India created this system in 1500 B.C., it was designed to divide the entire nation up into stratified groups based on the haves and have-nots. You were born into your group, which was rooted primarily in the Hindu beliefs about karma and reincarnation, and there was nothing you or anyone could do about it. The specific caste you were born into determined your people group, and it decided everything about your place in society.

India's Caste System. (Kwj2772)

Those at the top of the pyramid were considered the "haves", and they had it good. These were the Brahmins or Priest Class, followed by the Kshatriyas and Vaisyas. The caste system was designed to set up these top three tiers for success, but this came at the expense of the Shudras and another group called the Dalits who were relegated to the bottom of the pyramid. In fact, the Dalits (or "untouchables") actually existed outside the caste system and were considered *underneath* the very bottom. Those at the top had one experience in the nation, and those at the bottom had another completely different experience based on where they were on the pyramid – what was called their "social location". Those at the top benefited by keeping a certain segment of the population stuck at the bottom. These categories predetermined the jobs you could have, who you could marry and where you could live. This caste system ruled in India for 2,000 years until eventually a majority came to view it as unjust. In 1950, the system was made illegal and has not been enforced since. However, its impact on the nation is still very much visible and continues to be felt all throughout India. Despite the dissolution of the caste system, for the most part, the classes still exist in the social, psychological, and economic dynamics of the nation. Even today, the Dalits reside at the bottom of the hierarchy, unable to climb out of the hole their nation put them in so long ago[6]. This is ethnocentrism in one of its most destructive, widespread, and lasting forms.

A painfully similar dynamic of human division and separation also existed in the Rwandan crisis among African peoples. The three major groups in tension were the Hutu, Tutsi, and Twa peoples. The dynamics between these groups were unlike anything history had seen before.

The tension began at the end of World War I, when Belgium was in control of Rwanda, and introduced a permanent division of the population by classifying Rwandans into three ethnic groups based on race and physical features: Hutu, Tutsi, and Twa. To enforce this new Rwandan class system, Belgium gave out identity cards labeling each individual by group name. While it had previously been possible for wealthy Hutus to become honorary Tutsis, the new identity cards prevented any further movement between the groups and made socio-economic groups into permanent ethnic groups. As history tells it, Belgium appointed the minority (lighter-skinned and more "European-looking") Tutsi population to rule over the much larger Hutu population. Here is a breakdown of the groups by relative size and role:

> *Tutsi–15% Minority: held all the power and authority delegated by Belgium*
>
> *Hutu–84% Majority: had no power or authority*
>
> *Twa–1% Super-Minority: had no power or recognition by other groups*

The social dynamics created by this imposed and artificial class system led to immense tension between the different groups that built up over generations. This tension eventually exploded into a civil war in 1990 in which 800,000 people were killed. In this instance, the minority leveraged power over the majority, and it divided the people from one another[7].

Not all of ethnocentrism throughout history has been played out through war and conquest; some of it was just exhibited as pure hatred for the "other". We think of what the Nazis did to the Jewish people during the Holocaust, in which six million Jews were killed, or the conflict that arose in the early 1990's between the three main ethnic groups in Bosnia-Herzegovina: the Serbs, Croats and Muslims. In the latter conflict, over

200,000 Muslim civilian deaths were reported as a result of the "ethnic cleansing" that took place there, with an additional two million becoming refugees at the mercy of the Serbs, who were the group in power[8].

A simple Google search yields example after example of what we would consider modern-day genocides based on divisions between people groups.

There aren't many people who would try to make a case that these examples of human behavior aren't *wrong*. However, a closer look reveals there is something repetitive in the human experience where in our brokenness we continually drift into division and oppression and pridefully declare, "I am better than you." The Bible calls this prideful behavior sin, and sin always divides. It divides man from God and fellow man from one another. Romans 3:12 declares that all of us are susceptible to this condition of sin. This is the universal nature of our brokenness and it's been found on every shore on the Earth. Human beings, when left to our own devices, divide. And we will find that this divisive spirit – this ideology – even came to the shores of the great place we call America.

Questions for Reflection:

1. What strikes you about ethnocentrism as it has played out in various different nations?

   Each is unique yet the same

2. Where else have we seen ethnocentrism rise up in the world?

   USA – 175 yrs of it

3. Read Acts 10: 27 – 28 and verse 34. How does the concept of ethnocentrism show up in Peter's story? How did he respond when confronted with it?

   Under God's law all are one –

4. When have you noticed this feeling of "I'm better than other people" coming up in your own life?

   When I get into a discussion which that leads to an argument.

Chapter 3

A Long Time Ago in A Galaxy Far, Far Away...

I n order to see how ethnocentrism plays out even in our own country, we'll need to start back at our country's beginning. You might ask why we need to keep dredging up and examining the past, as many have in today's conversation about race. Many believe that focusing on the past just inspires more division. But in our pursuit for oneness and understanding, context is everything. Let's allow one of the most beloved movie sagas of all time to illustrate why history matters.

In 1977, George Lucas released a movie that would become a cultural and world phenomenon. He may not have known it at the time, but its blockbuster influence would continue here in the U.S. and around the world for at least another forty years into the future and beyond.

Many years after its initial release, generations born in the new millennium would adopt love for the epic tale of Star Wars! Almost everyone on the planet has heard of the Star Wars saga. It is a masterpiece!

Part of the genius of Star Wars was not just in how the story unfolded on the big screen with its groundbreaking visual effects, but the very specific storytelling technique that we, the audience, were thrust into. When we were introduced into the story of Star Wars, we did not start at the beginning; rather, we were transported right into the middle of the Star Wars story. Unbeknownst to us, the first Star Wars film in 1977 wasn't Episode One – it was Episode Four!

Not only did George Lucas drop us into the middle of the story, he also did not give us the full context or backstory. All we knew was what those words scrolling up the screen at the beginning of the movie told us, and in an instant, we were thrown into a massive universe of people and stories. We had to just go with it and do our best to make sense of it. We were so engulfed in the action that most of us didn't even think to question who was who, or what had led up to the confrontation on Princess Leia's ship in the opening scene of the film.

In that first Star Wars film, we were introduced to key players like Luke Skywalker, the young Jedi Knight who was instrumental in the resistance. We met Princess Leia, one of the leaders of the Imperial Senate. We met Han Solo and Chewbacca, two smugglers who charmed the screen with their out-of-this-world buddy chemistry.

We also met the character that many consider to be the most famous villain to ever appear on a movie screen: Darth Vader.

We were entranced by the menacing way he walked and talked, the stone-cold look of his face (okay, helmet) and the way he ruled with an iron fist. Vader was so powerful that he could destroy people without even touching them! We didn't fully understand where he was coming from, but we knew one thing for sure: Darth Vader was a bad dude no one wanted to cross paths with. We all could see the emotion and tension surrounding these characters, but there was very little context.

Over the following years, more episodes would be released. Moviegoers experienced one of the biggest shockers in movie history when Darth Vader said to Luke, "I am your father!" What?! And then the saga went silent for over a decade; no movies, no stories – we heard nothing.

Eventually it was announced that in May 1999, a new Star Wars trilogy was set to be released and would reveal the back-story...the events that took place *before* Leia, Luke, and Han were even born! The new trilogy was actually a prequel! As audience members, we got to see the rise and fall of Anakin Skywalker, a supremely talented natural-born Jedi Knight who unfortunately became more and more influenced by the dark side of the Force until it ended up taking him over and costing him not only the love of his life, but also his face and most of his limbs. Anakin became the villain we all loved to hate: Darth Vader.

Darth Vader's origin story turned what we thought about him on its head. We rooted for Anakin as a young slave boy in poverty, even knowing what he would eventually become. We watched him lose the only family he knew and grow up without a nurturing presence in his life. We saw him fall in love with Padme, and cheered for him as he fought the forces of evil alongside Obi Wan Kenobi. Eventually he started to lose his way, struggling to resist the dark side of the Force. The descent was painful to watch as much as it was inevitable. The crushing blow came when he learned of the death of his beloved Padme at the end of the second trilogy. We now had a fuller picture of Darth Vader. We could understand that he was motivated by his wounded heart, full of the pain of loss and intense feelings of betrayal.

While this knowledge doesn't change the fact that Darth Vader did some major bad-guy things (including blowing up a planet or two), we as the audience were able to develop a kind of empathy for his character and it would forever change how we saw the rest of the story play out. The fuller picture and back-story was crucial in understanding the whole story and its key players and events.

In many ways, this story illustrates and mirrors the gap in mutual understanding of our historical experience in America. Often when we are having the conversation around race we seem to start in different parts of the story. Some are focused on the here and now while others seem entrenched in the past. But what would happen if we truly examined *all* the parts of the story? Could it be that many of us really only know the middle? Many of us alive today are starting in "Episode Four" with no real motivation to understand the entire story – just the parts we can embrace. What would happen if we opened our hearts and minds up to the first part of the trilogy; the origin story of the lived experiences and events that came to shape the situation we find ourselves in today?

This book is predicated on the belief that knowing the full context of our shared story is key to mutual and authentic understanding, just as it was key to our deepened understanding of the Star Wars story.

The story of race relations in this country is teeming with events, players and circumstances, much of which have not been taught as part of a typical K through 12 education in the U.S. Essentially at this point in time, we've all been born into the middle of a story already taking place. And though none of us wrote or created it, we each get the opportunity to play important roles in how the next episodes play out.

If the story of America is now in "Episode Four", the question is: How much do we understand Episodes One, Two and Three? Could it be that those parts of the story are crucial to our mutual understanding? What if the story is fuller and much different than we previously knew? What if instead of pushing us further apart, a deeper understanding of the whole story drew us toward one another? Why wouldn't you want to know the full story? As believers in search of the truth, even though it can be uncomfortable and hard, learning more about our history is *not* about staying stuck in the past; it's what helps us navigate more knowledgeably in our *present.*

As we lean into the story of America and all of its episodes, what we discover in this vast saga will help us all find ourselves on the same page and prepare us to pursue Biblical oneness in a whole new way. If we're going to effectively be Christ's hands and feet in this crucial conversation with the goal of drawing people together, we need to understand what we're walking into. History is integral to seeing the present circumstances fully; otherwise, it's like walking into a situation full of conflict with a blindfold on. Avoiding a fuller understanding of the past puts us at a disadvantage and limits our ability to enter into the conversation around race in a meaningful way. In fact, many preachers of the Bible will tell you that understanding the context and history of any Bible passage is key to a greater understanding of the intended meaning of the original writers. Preachers are always going into the history of the Bible and the context of the passage.

Jesus also valued knowledge of history as an important component of growth. He often used historical context as He illuminated truth and enlightened his audiences. He knew history was important to being able to understand the present. Here is an example from Scripture. In it, Jesus referred to passages from Exodus, Leviticus, and Deuteronomy in order to move people forward in truth.

Matthew 5:38-44 (NIV)

[38] *"You have heard that it was said, 'Eye for eye, and tooth for tooth."*[39] *But I tell you, do not resist an evil person. If anyone slaps you on the right cheek, turn to them the other cheek also.* [40] *And if anyone wants to sue you and take your shirt, hand over your coat as well.* [41] *If anyone forces you to go one mile, go with them two miles.* [42] *Give to the one who asks you, and do not turn away from the one who wants to borrow from you.* [43] *"You have heard that it was said, 'Love your neighbor and hate your enemy.'* [44] *But I tell you, love your enemies and pray for those who persecute you,"*

Jesus was looking back to the historical context and understanding of how people treated one another and in doing so, He embraces that history and then illuminates a new way forward. Did you know that the book of the Bible that Jesus quotes most often during his public ministry is Deuteronomy? Conservative scholars believe that Deuteronomy was written by Moses around 1400 B.C.[9], meaning Jesus was repeatedly quoting a book written over a thousand years before his time. History was important then and still remains so today.

As we consider our own historical context in an effort to move forward in our nation, part of what Americans have universally wrestled with and disagreed on as part of the race conversation is the lasting impact of the way our nation began. It may be uncomfortable for some to talk about, but there is no disputing that America began as a nation dependent on the practice of slavery. In an article published in the Gilder Lehrman institute of American History, historian Steven Mintz asserts that looking at the economics alone, a strong case could be made that the development of America was heavily dependent upon slave labor. Here are some of his findings below:

"One crop, slave-grown cotton, provided over half of all U.S. export earnings. By 1840, the South grew 60 percent of the world's cotton and provided some 70 percent of the cotton consumed by the British textile industry. Thus slavery paid for a substantial share of the capital, iron, and manufactured goods that laid the basis for American economic growth. In addition, precisely because the South specialized in cotton production, the North developed a variety of businesses that provided services for the slave South, including textile factories, a meat processing industry, insurance companies, shippers, and cotton brokers."[10]

The North and South were in a codependent partnership with one another, each, directly or indirectly, benefitting from slavery. This played out primarily through the generational enslavement of Africans. This is our history.

However, there still seems to be disagreement surrounding the reality (or lack thereof) of any lasting impact of slavery, especially given that it was outlawed well over 150 years ago. Some argue that we need to move on. They say we've come so far, and they question the need to continue picking at the scabs of a healing wound. Meanwhile, others say we haven't yet effectively dealt with our history of slavery and its lasting impact.

The situation for African Americans in the U.S. today has certainly improved in recent decades. Although America is an incredible nation with many triumphs, it is also flawed just like every other nation on the planet. Equally as important as acknowledging our progress, we as a people need to have a similar understanding of the ways in which we as a nation have failed to move forward, and how these cycles of progress and backwards movement have contributed to the tensions we see today. What might be possible if we all checked our preconceived notions of the impact of slavery at the door and opened our minds and hearts to some new information? How might things improve if we better understood the backstory and context of the episode we are living in?

Questions for Reflection:

1. How important is Biblical history for Jesus? How important do you think it is for the believer?
   Jesus referred to it.

2. How important is Biblical history and context for a preacher? Ask one.

3. Read this scripture from Deuteronomy 4. What does it say about the importance of the past? How should we respond?
   Know the past, understand its relevance, Apply it
   Deuteronomy 4:9-10 (NIV) [9] *"Only be careful, and watch yourselves closely so that you do not forget the things your eyes have seen or let them fade from your heart as long as you live. Teach them to your children and to their children after them.* [10] *Remember the day you stood before the Lord your God at Horeb, when he said to me, "Assemble the people before me to hear my words so that they may learn to revere me as long as they live in the land and may teach them to their children."*

4. How important do you think it is to understand our nation's history in light of the conversation we are trying to have today? *Very impt. This topic encompasses a very large % of our country years existed*

5. Has there ever been a time where your view of an event or circumstance in your personal life changed once you discovered more information?

Chapter 4

America's Inheritance

M any successful books and movie scripts have included a scene where a character gets a sudden call that an unknown distant relative has died, and they have left a grand inheritance for their next-of-kin. What will be handed down and how will their lives change because of it? What is it about the idea of a windfall inheritance that can move us to imagine the same thing happening to *us* one day?

The truth is, we all have an inheritance. It may not be millions from a distant uncle; more likely it's your mother's charisma, your grandmother's legacy of prayer, your aunt's library of books, your father's natural athleticism. However, along with all the good things handed down to us, we may also inherit challenges. Did you inherit your mother's poor eyesight? Your grandfather's hot temper? Your family's predisposition for high blood pressure or depression? We certainly have no control of what is passed down to us, but we do have some control over how we manage and care for it.

America's inheritance is so rich. There are so many great things that this country has passed along to us, but we must also give attention to the challenging history of ethnocentrism we have inherited.

The universal pattern of cultural ethnocentrism is so prevalent in the human experience, its impact and implications so painful and long-lasting, it was inevitable that it would seep into the very foundation of our nation. We came by it honestly…by way of Europe. For centuries, Europe played out its own history of colonizing and imposing its culture in various parts of the world and so it was only a matter of time until it would arrive on the shores of a land already inhabited by a people group with its own unique culture – the land we refer to today as "America".

In 1492, a Catholic Italian explorer named Christopher Columbus reached what is now known as the Bahamas, accompanied by several vessels arriving from Spain. He had found the Americas. There are many speculations as to how and why he landed where he did, but the record is clear that he saw an opportunity for growth and expansion, which would ultimately be achieved at the expense of others. In recent years, this truth has been more and more understood, but it can also be hard for some to hear.

In his writings, Columbus journaled about the natives he encountered in the Americas, stating: "They ought to make good and skilled servants, for they repeat very quickly whatever we say to them. I think they can very easily be made Christians, for they seem to have no religion. If it pleases our Lord, I will take six of them to Your Highnesses when I depart, in order that they may learn our language."

He also wrote: "These people are very simple as in regards the use of arms, as your Highnesses will see from the seven that I caused to be taken, to bring home and learn our language and return; unless your Highnesses should order them all to be brought to Castile, or to be kept as captives on the same island; for with fifty men they can all be subjugated and made to do what is required of them…"[11]

It's easy to see that Christopher Columbus carried with him an ethnocentric view of the world, one where he and his nation sat at the top. Take note that as a Christian, he also didn't primarily identify natives as potential brothers and sisters to be won for Christ but as people to be brought into submission, subjection, and domination. He made the ethnocentric assumption that his culture and ways of life were better than what the Native Americans had already established for themselves.

It's important to note (and often missed) that Columbus' statement also gave us a clear window into his personal Christian theology. He saw Christianity as something to implement without paying any attention to "loving his neighbor as himself". He saw no conflict between the subjugation of other people and the tenets of his faith. His actions make clear that he didn't see any connection to the words of Jesus when He said that He "did not come to be served, but to serve, and to give his life as a ransom for many." Thus, he brought to America a distorted Christianity – one which utilized conversion as an instrument of European ethnocentric cultural advancement, not for the purposes of universal love, respect, or brotherhood that Jesus spoke so often about. The salvation power of the Gospel was completely missing from his words and actions towards those he deemed outsiders.

The sad irony is that his name, "Christopher", actually means Christ Bearer.[12]

Under Columbus' leadership, this ideological approach and world view would soon prevail as the general mindset of the Europeans that followed him to the "new" land. Unfortunately, this worldview would also take root in the American Church, saturating the air as we took our first collective breaths as a nation together. Many prominent early American ministers and preachers held very similar views and preached this distorted theology in their churches. As a result, European ethnocentrism became firmly established in America's DNA right from the start and would become a key component for the justification and implementation of the transatlantic slave trade.

Case in point: George Whitfield, a highly-influential Anglican clergyman and traveling evangelist who was one of the founders of the Methodist Church in America and the evangelical movement in general, held these views as well. Centuries later, you can hear the echoes of Columbus' ideas when Whitfield wrote on the subject of slavery:

"Give up the thought of seeking freedom from your masters. And though he [God] hath now called you into his own Family, to be his own Children and Servants; he doth not call you hereby from the Service of your Masters according to the Flesh; but to serve him in serving them, in obeying all their lawful Commands, and submitting to the Yoke his Providence has placed you under".[13]

Here's another excerpt from a letter written by Whitfield:

"The constitution of that colony [Georgia] is very bad, and it is impossible for the inhabitants to subsist without the use of slaves. But God has put it into the hearts of my South Carolina friends, to contribute liberally towards purchasing, in this province, a plantation and slaves, which I purpose to devote to the support of Bethesda. Blessed be God! The purchase is made. Last week, I bought, at a very cheap rate, a plantation of six hundred and forty acres of excellent ground ready cleared, fenced, and fit for rice, corn, and everything that will be necessary for provisions. One Negro has been given me. Some more I purpose to purchase this week."[14]

It is disheartening to say the least to realize that Whitfield penned the words quoted in the excerpts above as a pastor and co-founder of a Christian denomination. His influence was monumental. This European ethnocentric theology was also mainstreamed into the budding U.S. government.

You may already have learned as part of your education that many of our early presidents owned slaves, either during their presidency or outside of it. According to The White House Historical Association, these included George Washington, Thomas Jefferson, James Madison, James Monroe, Andrew Jackson, Martin Van Buren, William Henry Harrison, John Tyler, James K. Polk, Zachary Taylor, Andrew Johnson and Ulysses S. Grant.[15]

Some people give these founding fathers a pass on their slave ownership since, right or wrong, slavery was a generally-accepted practice at the time.

But how can we reconcile that with the seeming contradiction presented by these men, some of whom fought so hard for this country's freedom from a tyrannical English monarchy? Think about it. The same man who wrote "We hold these truths to be self-evident, that all men are created *equal*, that they are endowed by their creator with certain unalienable rights, that among these are life, liberty and the pursuit of happiness" also wrote "I advanced it, therefore, as a suspicion only, that the blacks, whether originally a distinct race, or made distinct by time or circumstances, are inferior to the whites in the endowments of both body and mind."

Both of these statements were written by Thomas Jefferson; the former in the Declaration of Independence in 1776 and the latter in his Notes on the State of Virginia, published in 1785.[16]

Even Abraham Lincoln, prior to famously mandating the emancipation of slaves, made the following remarks during one of a series of debates in 1858 with Stephen Douglas: "There is a physical difference between the white and the black races which I believe will forever forbid the two races living together... while they do remain together there must be the position of superior and inferior, and I as much as any man am in favor of having the superior position assigned to the white race." In the same speech Lincoln said: "I will say then that I am not, nor ever have been in favor of bringing about in any way the social and political equality of the white and black races." [17]

While we know what Lincoln went on to do with his Emancipation Proclamation (although his purpose in doing so is subject to some debate), we can see how the shadow of European ethnocentrism – the belief that white people were superior to black people – continued to loom large in the minds and hearts of our nation's earliest leaders. It is sobering to realize that even after revealing his thoughts on white versus black in 1858, Lincoln's election alone was viewed as threatening enough to the institution of slavery to trigger the events leading to the Civil War.

Questions for Reflection

1. What stands out to you about Christopher Columbus' words?

2. Re-read George Whitfield's statements about enslaved people. What do you notice?

3. What is the common thread between Christopher Columbus, George Whitfield, and the early Presidents?

4. How do you think the early church in America was affected by this theology?

Chapter 5

Ring Around the Rosie: Monumental Misunderstanding?

For generations of children growing up in America, "Ring Around the Rosie" has been one of those nursery rhyme hits we all knew by heart. "Ring around the Rosie pocket full of posies!" We would stand in a circle holding hands, turning in a circle waiting for the moment at the end when we would sing "We all fall down!"

At that moment we would all let go of each other's hands and fall to the floor. That was our favorite part! We all lay on the ground laughing in this fun childhood moment filled with so much joy. So many of us have this exact same memory. This is why it's difficult, shocking even, to learn the possible origin of this song.

Although there are many speculations about the origin, tradition holds that this nursery rhyme is about the Plague. The ring around the Rosie is likely referring to the circle-shaped rashes that broke out on the skin of those afflicted with the plague, and the pocket full of posies portray the flowers used to repel the pungent smells of the plague.[18]

You may feel a little less joy when reciting these lyrics now. Or at least marvel that you really didn't ever know what you were singing about!

Have you ever discovered more information about something and thought: "Wow! I had no idea it originated from that, or that other people saw it this way?"

Certainly, this phenomenon has happened in the battle of civil war monuments. Undoubtedly, you've seen images on TV of protests, marches, peaceful demonstrations and even some vandalism, especially since the death of George Floyd. These monuments have been a flash point of tension for the last several years.

In regard to the statues, on one side of the conversation are those who say: "This is our American history. Why be offended? The statues symbolize something honorable! We shouldn't forget history." While others wonder: "Do people really understand the message that these statues send to people of color and how they make some of them feel?" In essence, do we really know the full meaning behind these songs? This is a fair question: do we? How much do we know about the statues placed around us?

Take for example the largest Confederate monument in the United States located in Stone Mountain, Georgia. Etched into the stone of this memorial, which is a close rival of Mount Rushmore in South Dakota in terms of its size, are the likenesses of Stonewall Jackson and Robert E. Lee, two Confederate generals, and the President of the Confederacy, Jefferson Davis. There have been ongoing discussions on whether or not this monument should be removed.

Stone Mountain Memorial.
(Greg Balfour Evans/Alamy Stock Photo)

Some say it's common history and a part of America's heritage, so it needs to stay up. Why tear down history? Others say it's a reminder of slavery and an oppressive time in our nation's history, so they want it taken down. You may have friends and family on all sides of the issue, and you may even have strong feelings yourself.

I believe part of the dialogue includes understanding the origin of the monument, as it's actually not that old. The carving work first started in 1915 when someone came up with the idea to memorialize these men in stone in Georgia. The work hit some bumps in the road, and the carving work came to a grinding halt in the early 1920's. It wasn't until 1958, in a response to a sea-change in the U.S. Supreme Court when it came to issues of segregation (specifically, their ruling in Brown v. Board of Education in 1954 that segregation was unconstitutional), that

Georgia outright bought the land the unfinished carving was standing on and work began again in earnest in 1964. It took until 1972 for the memorial to be completed.[19] As it turns out, none of the three men in the carving are from Georgia.

So, what was the purpose of this massive memorial to three men who literally fought on the side of the Civil War battle to keep slavery alive and well in the United States of America? Let's also consider not just the battle they fought but statements and quotes made by the men on the monument.

In a letter Lee wrote to his wife in 1856, Lee shared his thoughts about the institution of slavery. "In this enlightened age, there are few I believe, but what will acknowledge, that slavery as an institution, is a moral & political evil in any Country." So far, so good, right?

But in that same letter, in regard to slavery in the U.S., he wrote that "The blacks are immeasurably better off here than in Africa, morally, socially & physically. The painful discipline they are undergoing is necessary for their instruction as a race, & I hope will prepare & lead them to better things. How long their subjugation may be necessary is known and ordered by a wise Merciful Providence."[20]

Lee knew right from wrong when it came to slavery, but somehow he was unable to walk in that conviction practically. He fought against a federal government that appeared to be leaning in an abolitionist direction and, per his own words, he even felt that slavery was a necessary tool of instruction for African Americans. This is what many people of color see when they look at these kinds of monuments.

However, this is only part of the picture. Now let's look at Jefferson Davis, the President of the Confederacy, and some of his quotes:

"We recognize the fact of the inferiority stamped upon that race of men by the Creator, and from the cradle to the grave, our Government, as a civil institution, marks that inferiority."[21]

"We recognize the negro as God and God's Book and God's Laws, in nature, tell us to recognize him. Our inferior, fitted expressly for servitude."[22]

It's these types of words that make it difficult for many people in our country to look up at these statues and to see anything other than those words. Certainly it was a different time and we've come a long way, but if the sight of these memorials hurt our own brothers and sisters, isn't a hard re-look at them worth it?

Let's look at another monument:

Emancipation Memorial in Washington, D.C.

This is the Emancipation Memorial. it was erected in 1876 in a project that was actually funded in part by newly-freed slaves. It was designed by artist Thomas Ball and was placed up in an effort to honor the moment freedom was granted to African Americans.[23]

However, after some reflection, there are those who wonder whether it needs to come down. Its replica statue was removed in Boston in 2020[24] and now there is a stir around the original one in Washington D.C.[25]

This monument, like many of the others, has created lots of tension in our nation, but the tension around this one is a little different, especially given the fact that this monument stands in a different category. For one thing, this statue is not a confederate monument and Lincoln is considered one of the greatest Presidents in our nation's history. He is viewed by many as a man whose leadership not only helped to end slavery, but for which he then went on to pay the ultimate price.

With all that being said, some of the tension around this statue, unlike some of the others (at least initially), may have more to do with the statue's appearance than anything else. What do you notice when you look at the statue? How does it make you feel? Recently it was revealed how Frederick Douglass felt about it in a recently discovered letter published in the National Republican:

"To the Editor of the National Republican:

Sir: Admirable as is the monument by Mr. Ball in Lincoln Park, it does not, as it seems to me, tell the whole truth, and perhaps no one monument could be made to tell the whole truth of any subject which it might be designed to illustrate. The mere act of breaking the negro's chains was the act of Abraham

Lincoln, and is beautifully expressed in this monument. But the act by which the negro was made a citizen of the United States and invested with the elective franchise was pre-eminently the act of President U. S. Grant, and this is nowhere seen in the Lincoln monument. The negro here, though rising is still on his knees and nude. What I want to see before I die is a monument representing the negro, not couchant on his knees like a four-footed animal, but erect on his feet like a man. There is room in Lincoln Park for another monument, and I throw out this suggestion to the end that it may be taken up and acted upon."[26]

Looking at his comments, it's clear that Frederick Douglass' issue with this statue has to do more with what is communicated through the body language it portrays than anything else. Abraham Lincoln is clearly in an intentional superior position towering above, while the other man is on his knees looking up. Can you see how this would not feel empowering to African Americans during that time or even today? If we are all made in the image of God and worthy of dignity, how does this statue sitting in a public park reflect that God-given identity that He placed in each of us?

The truth is that there are many statues and many issues to be worked through with each one. Should they stay to preserve civil war history and times past, or should they be removed in order to allow us to heal and move forward? Careful consideration is called for in the case of each statue and memorial.

As we close out this conversation. I would have you consider one last factor. One might say, 'But these memorials were erected by those who knew and loved these men – family members and comrades – to help assuage their grief at having lost their loved ones. The intent was not to celebrate their sin, as it were, but their bravery and integrity in fighting for freedom from an overreaching federal government. Looking at it this way, you might conclude that these memorials are just relics of the past, not significant enough to warrant a comprehensive program of removal.

But here's the truth: the bulk of the statues didn't go up right after the Civil War. They didn't even go up in the 1800's. Take a look at the graphic below. It's something the Southern Poverty Law Center published in their 2016 report entitled "Whose Heritage?". It graphs the erection of monuments, memorials, and schools honoring a person or event associated with the Confederacy over time. You might be surprised to see when the majority of them were erected:

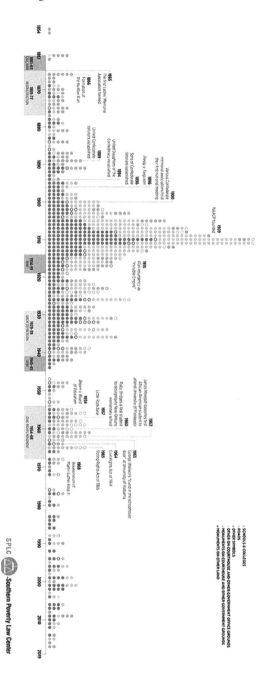

Courtesy of the Southern Poverty Law Center

From the report: "The dedication of Confederate monuments and the use of Confederate names and other iconography began shortly after the Civil War ended in 1865. But two distinct periods saw significant spikes. The first began around 1900 as Southern states were enacting Jim Crow laws to disenfranchise African Americans and re-segregate society after several decades of integration that followed Reconstruction. It lasted well into the 1920s, a period that also saw a strong revival of the Ku Klux Klan. The second period began in the mid-1950s and lasted until the late 1960s, the period encompassing the modern civil rights movement."[27]

As you can see, these memorials were essentially weaponized during periods of major disagreement around the equality question when it came to skin color. Many of them went up during times when those in power had overt intent in erecting them, to remind African Americans of the place they once held in history; that they were once slaves.

Questions for Reflection

1. How much was new information to you about the monuments? How many confederate monuments were erected in the state where you live now?

2. What are some visual reminders you've seen that indicate that perhaps the U.S. still has some ways to go in fully recognizing the wrongs of slavery?

3. What emotions does it bring up when you read some of the quotes and then see the images of the massive memorials erected to those who spoke them?

4. How might you approach this conversation differently now that you understand more of the context surrounding Confederate statues?

Chapter 6

What If?

Len Bias. (The Washington Post/Getty Images)

One can't help but ask the question: "What if?" after learning the story of Len Bias. What if this incredibly talented man would have been able to live a full life where he was able to reach his maximum potential? Len Bias was a bright and emerging star growing up in Hyattsville, Maryland whose love and passion for the game of basketball began to take root at a very young age.

Initially, Bias' potential wasn't fully realized as he wasn't even the first-picked player on his youth rec teams. However, as soon as he privately dedicated himself to perfecting his craft, the day would soon come when everyone would want to pick him first!

Bias went on to Northwestern High School where he excelled in basketball for four years and became a star. It was said that his jump shot rose straight up to the top, hovering in the clouds way above the outstretched hands of the helpless defenders. When he reached the height of his arc, he rained buckets on his opponents all day long. Everyone could see he was a force to be reckoned with, and he did it with an infectious smile.

When he stepped on the court, his skills always appeared to be a class above the competition. In fact, the summer before his freshman year at Maryland, Bias played in the Urban Coalition League, a summer league that was composed of elite college and local NBA players honing their skills in the off seasons. That summer, while still in high school, Bias dominated the league, scoring an average of 36 points per game. Pete Holbert, a junior at Maryland on the Terps basketball team, said that Bias was so good that he even outplayed the N.B.A players![28] He truly was incredible to see.

Bias went on to have four incredible seasons at Maryland, becoming the greatest scorer in their history, scoring 2,146 points. Bias went on to win ACC Player of the Year twice, and to date, he is still the only player in Terps history to accomplish that feat. His stats and his physical ability made him the most dominant player in all of college basketball. He was a once-in-a-generation talent. In 2003, Duke coach Mike Kryzewski said "This is my 24th year at Duke and in that time there have been two opposing players that really stood out: Michael Jordan and Len Bias."[29] The two of them in college had a great budding rivalry that many people couldn't wait to see carry over into the pros.

On June 17, 1986, Len Bias was drafted second in the first round of the NBA draft by the Boston Celtics. This incredible moment in his life would be the height of all his achievements thus far. It was a moment of great celebration, not just for Bias, but for the entire city of Boston as they were getting the very best collegiate athlete added to an already incredibly stacked Celtics team. Fans started talking of dynasties, future championships, and hyped-up rivalries.

But the celebrations would abruptly end just two days later, when Len Bias would tragically die from a drug overdose in his college dorm room. He was 22 years old.[29]

He never got to put his uniform on. He never signed one autograph as a professional player. He never played in a single NBA game. He never got to showcase his talent against the other greats in the league. Len Bias is the highest draft pick ever taken in the NBA draft to never play in a single game.

So much potential and so much promise, but we will never know what could have been.

We are left wondering "What if?"

In many ways, when one fully understands all the potential that was possible in America after the end of the Civil War, one might be tempted to ask: what if? What if all the promise and potential had been able to play out? What if?

You see, with the conclusion of the Civil War, the "Emancipation Proclamation '' set up an environment of new possibility for African Americans, one not available before, known as the "Reconstruction Era". Beginning in 1865 and lasting through the next twelve years, the challenge facing the

Federal government during this era was balancing the need to ensure that freedmen were actually able to enjoy their new-found rights with the goal of bringing the former Confederate states back into the Union fold. First, it opened the door for full freedom with the ratification of the 13th Amendment that officially ended slavery in the United States on Dec. 6, 1865.[30]

The rights granted to African Americans were subsequently expanded through further legislative efforts, federal laws, and constitutional amendments. The Fourteenth and Fifteenth Amendments added citizenship rights and the constitutional right to vote, respectively, although the latter was only granted to African American men. The newly-freed people seemed to be on their way.

In addition to this, African Americans could now also own property, legally marry, and receive an education in the United States. In fact, with the help of the Freedmen's Bureau alone, 200,000 former slaves learned to read.[31]

For the first time, African Americans could form families, settle down and live without the constant threat of familial separation from loved ones and children through sales and auctions. During this period of time, many African Americans also traveled for the first time. Some went to new cities seeking new opportunities vocationally and some went seeking to close gaps relationally looking for lost family members. It was clear immediately with the end of slavery that African Americans had discovered a new way of life, where the future seemed bright. The ideals of America seemed to be just within reach.

One of the greatest and almost immediate accomplishments for African Americans was realized politically. In fact, in the year 1868, 700,000 African Americans were registered to vote. This formed a new powerful voting block that helped to put

17 African Americans in the United States Congress, 15 in the House of Representatives, and two in the Senate. In fact, some historians estimate that by 1877 about 2,000 African American men had won local, state, and federal offices in the former Confederate states.[32]

One political standout during this time was Hiram Rhodes Revels:

Hiram Rhodes Revels.

Hiram was born a free man in Fayetteville, North Carolina. His father was an African American and his mother was of Scottish descent. In 1870, voters would elect Hiram as the first African American Senator. Reflecting on Hiram's election, a fellow senator named Charles Sumner remarked: "All men are created equal, says the great Declaration, and now a great act attests this verity. Today we make the Declaration a reality. The Declaration was only half established by Independence. The greatest duty remained behind. In assuring the equal rights of all we complete the work."[33]

This was an important moment for all Americans as this new freedom was a testament to the very words America was built on. Despite the tension that preceded his election, Hiram was said to be greeted into the senate chambers with great applause that day and for the first time, the freedom that was promised in the Declaration of Independence seemed to be in reach of all Americans. Consider the power of this moment in that it occurred just five years removed from the conclusion of institutionalized slavery in America. This was an incredible feat by the standards and practices that preceded this and no doubt for African Americans it seemed to signal a new day as there were achievements in all areas of life: economically, educationally, and politically. But sadly, many would soon realize that the cheering would stop and many of these freedoms and achievements would quickly grind to a halt.

Unfortunately, the 1876 presidential election precipitated the downfall of the Reconstruction Era. Returns from the three southern states were disputed, and in order to resolve the issue, a compromise was struck – Rutherford B. Hayes would be granted the election win contingent upon the removal of all remaining federal troops in the South. As the last of the federal troops evacuated in 1877, backlash and violent extremism began to dominate the South as African Americans no longer had federal protection to ensure their safety or the protection of any rights. As a result, voting rights for African American men in the former Confederate states were strategically restricted by poll taxes, literacy tests, intimidation, violence and fraud. The gains made by African Americans began to erode and this was only the beginning.

The infamous "grandfather clause" protected illiterate White men, allowing anyone who's grandfather was qualified to vote prior to the Civil War to be registered. Of course, this excluded all African Americans.

So African Americans were still free but now not able to vote. In fact, things deteriorated to the point where another African American would not be elected to the senate until 92 years later, when Senator Edward Brooke of Massachusetts took office in 1967.[34]

In addition to this, property was stripped, job opportunities and education opportunities were limited, and as a result, African Americans began to drift as a people into poverty and despair. In fact, for the next hundred years, blacks would endure a painful struggle for federal recognition of racial equality until the passing of the Civil Rights Act in 1968, which outlawed racial discrimination federally in the United States.[35]

Looking back on the Reconstruction Era, W.E.B. Du Bois wrote in 1935, "The slave went free; stood a brief moment in the sun; then moved back again toward slavery."[36]

When one looks at the achievements that were budding and all that was happening at the start of the Reconstruction period, one can only wonder: What if all of this potential had been allowed to play out? Where would we be today as Americans? What if?

Questions for Reflection:

1. What do you think would've happened had Reconstruction been allowed to continue? What do you think would be different today?

2. Please read the Scripture verse below. How does it speak to God's heart regarding the situation African Americans found themselves in in America?

Jeremiah 29:11

For I know the plans I have for you," declares the Lord, "plans to prosper you and not to harm you, plans to give you hope and a future.

3. What do you think you would see today that would be different in our country if all of this progress had been able to play out?

4. How do you think it felt not being able to vote in your own country?

5. What does Scripture say about the equality of all people?

Chapter 7

"Sorry, you didn't read the fine print."

Have you ever gotten so excited about closing the deal on buying something new? You were so ready to buy that house, drive that car, or cook with that new appliance, but then you're handed a tedious contract with pages of terms and conditions that you have to agree to. It's the infamous "fine print". This often happens even when just signing up for the latest smartphone app; these companies want us to sign the terms and conditions before moving ahead. The truth is these agreements are often so long and overwhelming that hardly anybody reads them, and so we skip right over reading through and we scroll right down to the bottom of the screen and hit "ACCEPT", trusting that everything is going to be just fine.

Sadly, it's only after the moment that we sign our names or click 'accept' that those hidden details, loopholes, and other issues with your contract could emerge. When your new prized possession starts acting up or breaks down, all of a sudden you find yourself revisiting all that seemingly meaningless paperwork. You start searching through the fine print.

Sometimes it's in the small details that bigger consequences or true motives are revealed. This is the reason for the saying "Always read the fine print," because you never know what's buried within. It may not be as good a deal as previously presented.

When it comes to the Civil War and why it was fought, we have a case where there was something buried in the fine print. On the surface, it seemed as though a new day of freedom and equality had dawned, but underneath all the rhetoric about freedom there was something lurking in the fine print that would be revealing of the hearts of men.

Based on our history lessons in grade school, one could easily conclude that the Civil War was fought for the freedom and equality for African-Americans – that the ending of the War marked a new moment when all people – regardless of skin color–were now free to pursue the American dream. At the start of the Reconstruction Era this seemed to be the case.

However, when looking closer at the details of the context of that time and the behaviors that followed, it turns out there was something in the fine print.

Let's revisit these quotes from earlier with this content now in front of us.

The Declaration of Independence states: "We hold these truths to be self-evident, that all men are created equal, that they are endowed by their creator with certain unalienable rights, that among these are life, liberty and the pursuit of happiness."

This is a great quote, one that many wanted to reach for after the Civil War. Sadly, what gets revealed in the details is that this idea didn't apply to everyone. The fine print was that our nation's leaders had a different view of equality that gets revealed in quotes below:

"I advanced it, therefore, as a suspicion only, that the blacks, whether originally a distinct race, or made distinct by time or circumstances, are inferior to the whites in the endowments of both body and mind."[37]

~THOMAS JEFFERSON (Founding Father,
3rd President of United States)

"We have, as far as possible, closed every avenue by which the light may enter the slave's mind. If we could extinguish the capacity to see the light, our work will be complete. They would then be on the level of the beast of the fields and we then should be safe."[38]

~HENRY BERRY (Virginia House of Delegates)

"There is a physical difference between the white and the black races which I believe will forever forbid the two races living together... while they do remain together there must be the position of superior and inferior, and I as much as any man am in favor having the superior position assigned to the white race."[39]

In the same speech: "I will say then that I am not, nor ever have been in favor of bringing about in any way the social and political equality of the white and black races."[40]

~ABRAHAM LINCOLN
(16th President of the United States)

Consider these statements by the man who many of us have been taught was a proponent of new ideas on race in America in his day. If these were his views on African American equality and he was the architect of the Emancipation Proclamation, then, whatever Lincoln's motivations were in ending the institution of slavery, it's clear that actual equality was not even a consideration at this point.

Abraham Lincoln could not fathom the idea of an African American being equal to him. This is important to understand because it helps us see the subsequent policies and practices that showed up after slavery ended in a new light. Slavery ended, but the idea of superiority didn't, and legislators in the coming years would reflect and codify that idea into law.

All of this took place in a time when white men widely read the Bible and knew the Exodus story of God's liberation of the Jewish people from the oppression of the Egyptians. They knew of Exodus 6:6-7 (NIV) which proclaims:

> [6] *"Therefore, say to the Israelites: 'I am the Lord, and I will bring you out from under the yoke of the Egyptians. I will free you from being slaves to them, and I will redeem you with an outstretched arm and with mighty acts of judgment. [7] I will take you as my own people, and I will be your God. Then you will know that I am the Lord your God, who brought you out from under the yoke of the Egyptians."*

They knew all of this, but they failed to apply that understanding to what was happening in America under their own leadership. In essence, advancing one culture became more important than advancing the kingdom principles they read about in the Bible.

This, my friends, is what was in the fine print. African Americans were set free from slavery but lived in a country that still did not recognize their human equality. The fine print was still being revealed in subsequent decades after Reconstruction.

Black Codes & Jim Crow Policies

The codes and policies referred to above were designed to crush most, if not all, of the gains made by African Americans under the Reconstruction Era. These were a series of oppressive laws and tactics used to disenfranchise and segregate African-American people – laws which touched every area of their lives.

Among other things, these laws prohibited intermarrying with a white person (a felony charge with a life sentence in Mississippi), freely changing jobs (freedmen had to forfeit any wages earned from the start of their contract up to the day of quitting), and owning firearms, ammunition, or weaponry in the form of knives (unless the person of color had a special license not required of their white counterparts). Besides these examples, African Americans could also be arrested for such things as "malicious mischief" and "insulting gestures, language, or acts" (also Mississippi).[40]

Perhaps most impactful, however, were the codes having to do with vagrancy. These laws made it illegal to be homeless and/or jobless. Yes, laws like this had existed in some form all over the world for hundreds of years, but think about the impact of such a law on 3.5 million newly-freed individuals – all of whom, in an instant more or less, became homeless and jobless. Essentially, the vagrancy laws required African Americans to be gainfully employed or they could be arrested and literally leased out to anyone willing to pay a fee to the state...a practice called "Convict Leasing". These laws sadly reveal that equality was not an option for African Americans and that there was a strategic, unyielding, and sustained effort to push them to the bottom of society.[41]

In subsequent years, this inequality would further be codified through Jim Crow laws which existed from the 1870's–1965. These laws below were legally enforced in the United States of America. Here are several below[43]:

Alabama

Nurses: No person or corporation shall require any white female nurse to nurse in wards or rooms in hospitals, either public or private, in which negro men are placed.

Restaurants: It shall be unlawful to conduct a restaurant or other place for the serving of food in the city, at which white and colored people are served in the same room, unless such white and colored persons are effectually separated by a solid partition extending from the floor upward to a distance of seven feet or higher, and unless a separate entrance from the street is provided for each compartment.

Pool and Billiard Rooms: It shall be unlawful for a negro and white person to play together or in company with each other at any game of pool or billiards.

Mississippi

Education: Separate schools shall be maintained for the children of the white and colored races.

Promotion of Equality: Any person...who shall be guilty of printing, publishing or circulating printed, typewritten or written matter urging or presenting for public acceptance or general information, arguments or suggestions in favor of social equality or of intermarriage between whites and negroes, shall be guilty of a misdemeanor and subject to fine not exceeding five hundred (500.00) dollars or imprisonment not exceeding six (6) months or both.

Prisons: The warden shall see that the white convicts shall have separate apartments for both eating and sleeping from the negro convicts.

Even in more northern states like Maryland these policies were enacted:

Maryland[42]

Intermarriage: All marriages between a white person and a negro, or between a white person and a person of negro descent, to the third generation, inclusive, or between a white person and a member of the Malay race; or between the negro and a member of the Malay race; or between a person of Negro descent, to the third generation, inclusive, and a member of the Malay race, are forever prohibited, and shall be void.

Railroads: All railroad companies and corporations, and all persons running or operating cars or coaches by steam on any railroad line or track in the State of Maryland, for the transportation of passengers, are hereby required to provide separate cars or coaches for the travel and transportation of the white and colored passengers.

I share this because most of us did not see this growing up in grade school or even in college and so it becomes important for us to look at this as we move toward one another in conversation so that we have a shared understanding of what preceded us. The social policies of that day facilitated an environment in which African Americans were continually treated unequally but this isn't limited to just social policies. These ideas buried in the fine print would also play out as well in the media and the entertainment world.

Sadly, there was "The Strange Tale of Ten Little Nigger Boys", a children's novel published in 1900. In addition to its offensive title, this book depicted a demeaning and degrading view of African-Americans filled with stereotypes[43]. Considering that young children were presumably consuming this content along with others of its kind, imagine how this shaped our collective thinking seeing this type of negative portrayal circulated as entertainment.

And there was live theater, too: "The minstrel show, or minstrelsy, was an American form of racist entertainment developed in the early 19th century. Each show consisted of comic skits, variety acts, dancing, and music performances that depicted people specifically of African descent. The shows were performed by mostly white people in make-up or blackface for the purpose of playing the role of black people. There were also some African-American performers and black-only minstrel groups that formed and toured. Minstrel shows lampooned black people as dim-witted, lazy, buffoonish, superstitious and happy-go-lucky."

"The form survived as professional entertainment until about 1910; amateur performances continued until the 1960s in high schools and local theaters."[44]

These depictions sought to dehumanize and belittle people of color. Tragically, there were even darker images that emerged during this same time period – images that went way beyond demeaning. This played out in theological circles as well with a book called "The Negro A Beast Or In The Image of God".

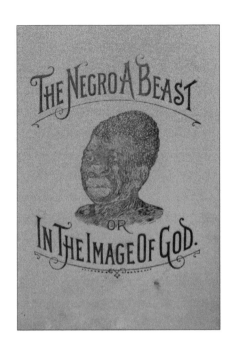

This book was a theological work written by Charles Carroll, a slave owner. Charles begins his book basically posing the question: are African Americans beasts, or are they made in the image of God? In this book Jesus is depicted as a European and then the case is made that if Jesus looks a certain way, with European features and African Americans look another way, then surely they can't be his offspring. Carroll spends 382 pages trying to support this argument.[45] This book had a positive reception in the culture of the time and even in the American Church. We've come an incredibly long way since then and it is important to know the way from which we came.

Finally, there is the sad story of Ota Benga. His story, even given the cultural climate of the times, seems unbelievable. "(He) was a Mbuti (Congo pygmy) man, known for being featured in an exhibit at the 1904 Louisiana Purchase Exposition in St. Louis, Missouri, and as a human zoo exhibit in 1906 at the Bronx Zoo. Benga had been purchased from African slave traders by the explorer Samuel Phillips Verner, a businessman searching for African people for the exhibition, who took him to the United States. While at the Bronx Zoo, Benga was allowed to walk the grounds before and after he was exhibited in the zoo's Monkey House."[46]

Ota Benga. (Library of Congress, Prints & Photographs Division (LC-B2-3971-2 [P&P])

An African American girl on exhibit at the "People's Show".

This story was so tragic and demeaning for all Americans and extremely hurtful to Ota himself. In July, 2020, the Bronx Zoo did formally apologize for putting Ota Benga on display in the zoo.[47]

While the story of Ota Benga might represent an isolated occurrence, the regular depiction of black people as evil and/or ignorant unfortunately was not, and these depictions would play out in the media, advertisements, books, and TV for decades to come. These depictions would send the message yet again that African Americans were set free from the chains of slavery in America, but equality with their fellow man was not part of the deal. This was the fine print. And while this tragic part of the American story may feel isolated to our nation, the truth is, it is not. On every continent there has been the temptation for one culture to diminish another. The root of this behavior is sin and this is the very thing Jesus came to treat in each and every one of us.

Questions for Reflection:

1. How do you think Ota Benga's display in the zoo made African Americans feel during that time? What do you think the psychological impact was on black and white children?

2. Have you ever felt the sting of being treated unfairly, or felt you were misrepresented? What feelings or actions did this produce in you?

3. What stories in Scripture come to mind as you read this chapter?

Chapter 8

The Redlining of Joe Louis

Joe Louis. (Gamma-Keystone/Getty Images)

I t might be hard for us to imagine, but in 1938, Joe Louis was hands down the single most popular athlete in the world. At the young age of twenty-four he had risen to a pinnacle of fame only understood in our contemporary minds when compared to the likes of Michael Jordan or LeBron James. But Joe's star rose even higher. Joe Louis fought during a time when boxing was not just the number one professional sport in the United States, but in the world; and Joe Louis stood at the top for a very long time as a champion.

His greatest moment of fame came when he squared off in a rematch against German boxer Max Schmeling in 1938. This was a rematch to the first fight two years prior where Joe Louis lost for the first time. In that fight, Schmeling knocked Joe out in the 12th round.

The rematch was set and the stakes were high, especially in the context of a world heading into WW2. The German Nazi regime was creating worldwide tension that would implode into world war.

With this as a backdrop, Joe Louis was marketed as America's champion and Max Schmeling stood as Germany's during Hitlers reign. The significance of the upcoming bout took on mythical proportions as a surrogate battle between Good America and Evil Germany. A record 70,000 people flooded Yankee Stadium and 100 million people tuned in on the radio, making it the largest sporting event ever at the time.

Joe stepped into the ring in perfect form, ready to seize the moment. The entire nation cheered as Joe went toe to toe with Max Schmeling. Joe was poised and set to go as soon as the bell rang and this time the result would be different. As Joe Louis landed blow after blow, he went on to knock out Max Schmeling in the first round of the fight. The crowd erupted in ecstatic praise for him as he claimed victory. When Joe won, America won. It was the first time the entire nation cheered for a black athlete to win.[48]

It was an important moment for our country and an important moment for African Americans. Joe was a national hero.

Joe often donated his proceeds to charity, and following that fight, Joe donated much of his winnings to help continued war efforts. Some estimates suggest Louis donated, if equivalent to current times, over $1.2 million during his career.

Joe went on to win many more prizefights until he hung up his gloves in 1948. In retirement, Louis set out to seek investments for his prize money in an effort to create wealth for his family. Joe decided he wanted to sell cars, so he reached out to the Ford Motor Company in an effort to buy himself a Ford dealership.

Joe met personally with CEO Henry Ford II and made his request to buy a dealership. Ford then tasked their sales team to test the waters to see how the idea resonated among car dealers and managers across the country. For, if this was approved, Joe Louis would be the first black person to own a Ford dealership.

The response was unanimous. The proposal was denied and the feedback warned of the backlash to the idea of a black man owning a car dealership. Joe was denied the opportunity to invest his wealth in one of the finest companies the world had to offer.[49]

Sadly, Joe struggled to find opportunities to invest his wealth in other places as well because the social norms of the land hindered black people from business ownership in many arenas. Louis eventually fell on hard times. He got into trouble with the IRS, got addicted to drugs, and went bankrupt.

The last job Joe held was serving as a greeter at Caesar's Palace in his senior years. Joe Lewis passed away in 1981 completely broke. Much of his money he gave away to charity, but was unable to pay the taxes on it because donations were not tax deductible in his day.[50]

On the other hand, remember Max Schmeling? Upon his retirement, as a German citizen, he was able to buy a Coca-Cola plant – one of the top American companies. He invested significant money into his business and made a large profit.[51] Max lived quite comfortably to a ripe old age while Joe Louis, the man who fought for democracy, died a broke greeter at Caesar's palace. He was strategically denied the ability to invest by Ford; denied the opportunity to succeed in the very country he fought for.

While we don't know the magnitude of the role this played on Joe ending up in poverty, we do know it played a part. Because at a time when he had the resources to build his wealth and invest in the capitalist idea of America, where one could be anything they wanted to be, he was told no.

In fact, every African American was told no and not a single African American was able to own a Ford dealership until over twenty years later after the Civil Rights Bill was passed in 1968, making racial segregation, discrimination, and disenfranchisement illegal. But the damage was already done because at the time the industry was taking off and creating tremendous wealth opportunities in the nation, African Americans were completely excluded from involvement in the process. These effects are still seen today as less than 1.5% of car dealerships are owned by African Americans.[52]

Therefore, we can ascertain, not only was Joe denied the ability to succeed, so were generations of African Americans through discriminating policies and social norms. Joe was denied the opportunity to succeed and directed toward less desirable options. He was essentially railroaded and directed into poverty. But this was not the only place these policies of exclusion from opportunity existed. In fact, they would touch an even bigger economic avenue and cause an even bigger chasm of disenfranchisement: in real estate.

Home Ownership

Part of what we end up seeing is that this was a pattern of wholesale discrimination that played out in America in more than just the car dealership business. It also played out on some level in home ownership, all the way up until racial discrimination was made illegal in 1968.

Home ownership is one of the biggest ways to develop, build and transfer wealth in the United States of America. This industry like all the others fell victim to racial discrimination and what many don't realize is the huge part that played in creating some of the challenges that we see today.

The entire housing industry had an array of policies aimed at controlling who got access to financing, who lived in the best neighborhoods, and who got directed toward less desirable areas – and it was all based on race. These policies did not operate under the cloak of night; they were being created and facilitated by the United States government out in the open. Race-restricted covenants and "redlining" were both tools sanctioned by the federal government and used by the real estate industry in various municipalities to prevent the "encroachment" of people of color and other "undesirable" people groups into majority white neighborhoods.[53]

Race-restrictive covenants were rules found in deeds to real property that disallowed the owner of the property from permitting use or occupancy to people based on religion or ethnicity. By the 1920's they were used to enforce racial segregation in towns and cities throughout the country and it wasn't until

1948 that the Supreme Court ruled that covenants of this type could no longer be enforced (Shelley v. Kramer).[54]

The Federal Housing Administration ("FHA") was created in 1934 as part of FDR's New Deal to help bolster the struggling housing market, primarily by protecting lenders by insuring the mortgage loans they made to home buyers. Its Underwriting Manual required lenders to keep on file something called "residential security maps" to guide them in their lending decisions – green shading for highly desirable newer areas (typically more wealthy neighborhoods in the suburbs), blue shading for established but less affluent areas (i.e., a little less desirable for lending), and yellow shading for neighborhoods on the decline (not desirable for lending).

Meanwhile, red shading was reserved for older neighborhoods, usually in the middle of cities and these are the areas that African Americans left the South and flocked to in search of jobs. These were urban centers like New York City, Detroit, Chicago, Cleveland, and the like. Based on these policies, African Americans were limited to living in these areas whether they wanted to or not.[55]

Here is a copy of a redlining map from the city of Brooklyn:

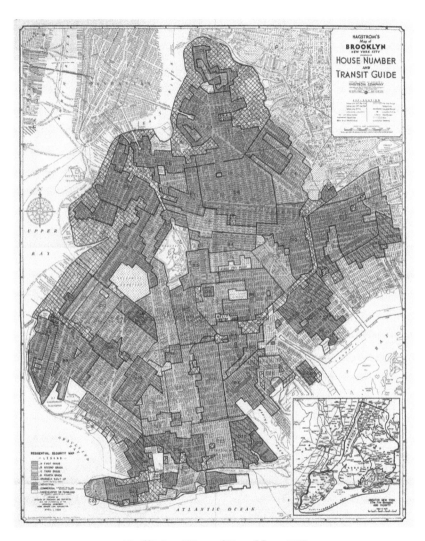

Redlining Map of Brooklyn, NY.

Based on the fact that loans were all but automatically rejected for areas shaded in red, regardless of stated intent, these maps were effectively used to discriminate against people of color in the practice that came to be called "redlining". Some of the evidence of this practice is the statistic that shows that black people received less than 2% of all federally-insured home loans between 1946 and 1959. Again, regardless of intent, the policy effectively excluded African Americans from being able to secure mortgage loans.[56]

And remember, it's not like people of color could just move to areas that weren't shaded in red. The race-restricted covenants mentioned earlier made this all but impossible. The rationale for these covenants is partially explained in this quote from a 1938 FHA publication in Section 9, Paragraph 937:

"Areas surrounding a location are investigated to determine whether incompatible racial and social groups are present, for the purpose of making a prediction regarding the probability of the location being invaded by such groups. If a neighborhood is to retain its stability, it is necessary the properties shall continue to be occupied by the same social and racial classes. A change in social or racial occupancy generally contributes to instability and decline in values."

Section 9, Paragraph 980 (3) recommends the use of recorded restrictive covenants which include provisions for, among other things, "g. Prohibition of the occupancy of properties except by the race for which they are intended".[57]

These kinds of policies made the amazing benefits of the GI Bill, which entitled war veterans to a business or home loan insured by the Veterans Administration, all but non-existent for African American veterans. Records show that between 1944 and 1955, while there were 1.1 million black veterans coming out of World War II, only approximately 30,000 (or 0.7%) of the 3.9 million VA-backed home loans were given to African Americans.[58]

These types of attitudes, rules, policies, and practices effectively trapped African Americans in less affluent neighborhoods, where property values were in decline or already low. In a never-ending downward spiral, these conditions drove those with the financial ability to do so *out* of those neighborhoods…and small local businesses followed. Many of those neighborhoods are still struggling today. These policies not only hurt impoverished neighborhoods and kept the people living in them unable to secure financing needed to move out of them. They also created barriers to economic investment, growth, and the ability to build legacy wealth through inheritance for the greater part of the 20th century for African Americans, just as discriminatory policies did to Joe Louis. Consider that the real estate market is one of the most profitable markets in the world and African Americans were legally excluded from it. Thankfully, redlining is now illegal in all 50 states, but unfortunately, its damaging footprint on American neighborhoods can still be seen in every place it existed. After decades of these policies being implemented by law, they have helped create the foundation for many of the struggling communities we still see today.

Questions for Reflection:

1. What did you think of the contrast between Joe Louis and Max Schmeling and how they were treated when it came to business opportunities?

2. Where can you see the effects of redlining in American neighborhoods today?

3. In what areas did it exist in your state and how are those neighborhoods doing today?

Chapter 9

Personal Responsibility vs. Outside Circumstances

As we look at some of the challenges we see today in urban areas (poverty, crime, struggling schools, etc.) the question that often comes up when discussing fixing many of these challenges is: are the solutions really about personal responsibility or outside circumstances?

For a moment imagine something horrible: you've sailed forty miles out to the middle of the ocean and suddenly you've been thrown overboard with no life preserver. The boat pulls off and leaves you there. Picture the vessel floating away from you until it becomes a dot on the horizon. How long would you last in that ocean?

As you begin to struggle, your efforts may do some good to keep you afloat, but eventually you'll run out of energy and drown unless someone from the outside helps you save yourself. Can a drowning person save themselves? Not in that situation. This same concept has played itself out in many communities in our nation. So many people are drowning in circumstances that, to some extent, they have been sucked into by the roots of

America's past and now these same people are being asked to save themselves from the rising waters based on their own character and efforts. This can be nearly impossible without outside help. Healing many of the cyclical struggles we see today will require compassion, leadership, and aid to those in struggling circumstances.

Coming full circle, however, although it is true that many times a drowning man cannot often save himself, it is certainly most helpful if he has a will and desire to assist or help in his own saving. Each of us must take responsibility for our own actions and do our best in the circumstances we find ourselves in until they change. Regardless of our circumstances or situations, we simply can't give up. Most of the rhetoric we're seeing today in the media (mainstream or otherwise) and on message boards/social media platforms have an "either/or" approach as was alluded to in the Introduction to this book. I'm sure you've noticed that while one side tends to look to lack of personal discipline and responsibility as the heart of the problem, the other side tends to blame outside circumstances for the bulk of the issues. As mentioned earlier, the answer lies somewhere in the middle. We need both.

Maybe you are one who believes personal responsibility is the most relevant factor to this discussion. Indeed, personal responsibility plays a HUGE role in this conversation. Scripture tells us that we will each have to give an account of ourselves before God in the end. We won't have our attorney with us; we won't have a power-point presentation showing how most of our bad decisions weren't our fault. Scripture repeatedly teaches that we are each responsible for our own thoughts and actions. We are not to blame others for our own shortcomings.

Both the second letter to the Corinthians and Paul's letter to the Romans speak to this:

2 Corinthians 5:10 (NIV): *"For we must all appear before the judgment seat of Christ, so that each of us may receive what is due us for the things done while in the body, whether good or bad."*

Romans 14:10 (NIV): *"You, then, why do you judge your brother or sister? Or why do you treat them with contempt? For we will all stand before God's judgment seat."*

However, many of us have a tendency to judge a person's struggles and challenges based on what *our own* struggles and unique challenges have been. Many of us like to think that if *we* had been Eve, we *never* would have taken a bite out of that apple. It's a natural human response to want to think that we would rise above in a challenge where someone else has not. Indeed, many people of ALL skin colors *have* risen above some of the hardest things any man has ever endured. This includes Job, of course, but it also includes the kid growing up in Appalachia with no money and the person with the debilitating life-long health problems. We have all heard unbelievable stories of people overcoming adversity.

So it can be tempting to look at the kind of disparities we see in income, wealth, homeownership, and other measures of success and think that somehow it must be the *person's* fault. We look at our "color-blind" laws in this country…the country of opportunity…and our society tells us that everyone has a chance to be whatever they want to be…as long as they have the discipline, the strength, and the perseverance to do what it takes.

But it's ALSO important to think about what outside factors influence our everyday decisions in life: things like your family unit, where you live, what school you went to, how much money you make, and what messages you've received from the surrounding culture at large. This isn't to the exclusion of personal effort and responsibility, it's *in concert* with those concepts. And some of these outside factors, while they can seem like ancient history to those of us who haven't been affected by them, are like just *yesterday* to someone who has been. Some of the policies that our nation enforced by codifying discrimination into law have had a devastating impact on generations of people and still have damaging effects that we need to continue to heal today. These policies are not as far removed in time as we might like to treat them as a nation. It bears repeating: we can be tempted to dull the sting by characterizing these times as ancient past.

Consider Ruby Bridges and her incredible story. Just as the U.S. Supreme Court turned the corner on segregation issues in 1954 by ruling that school segregation violated the Constitution and the modern-day Civil Rights movement got underway, Ruby made her appearance in the world. The Supreme Court ruling in the Brown v. Board of Education case meant that schools were now federally mandated to work towards integration over a six-year span.

However, the federal mandate met with steep resistance from states in the South. The resistance was often mob-oriented and prone to violence. In some instances, federal troops or marshals had to escort African American children to integrated schools.

On November 14, 1960, Ruby would become one of those children as she walked to her first day at the all-white William Frantz Elementary School in Louisiana. She is pictured here.

Ruby Bridges being escorted to William Frantz Elementary School.

This was an important moment for our nation. Sadly, as powerful as that moment was, it was still a symbol for what could be and what was not yet. When she walked into school that day, Ruby was alone because every single parent had withdrawn their children in protest. Not only that, but only one teacher, Barbara Henry, agreed to actually instruct Ruby. This one-on-one instruction continued for the entire school year.[59]

While this black and white image may seem like a scene from ancient history, it is not.

Below is Ruby's portrait from 2021. She looks like she could be your co-worker, friend, neighbor, someone at the grocery store and yet we could not possibly imagine what she has seen and endured.

Ruby Bridges in 2021. (Infrogmation of New Orleans)

There are millions of Americans alive today who attended legally segregated schools. In fact, my own mother attended a segregated school for most of her childhood. For younger generations, segregation feels as remote as the trends of poodle skirts and saddle shoes. But this wasn't generations ago. Dear reader, this may have been your grandmother, your father. It could have been you. Imagine how this must've felt. The psychological and emotional ramifications this had on many young Americans aren't ancient history. This discriminatory policy has had lasting impact that is present today. Many of the struggles we see today in certain communities are connected to the past struggles of those communities. The effect of the disenfranchisement and discrimination policies of our past is still playing out right before our eyes. This is not ancient history. Our historical challenges are closer to us and have a greater impact on what we see today than we were often taught in grade school. Therefore, I believe we must take ownership of some of what preceded us and do our best to help lift others up even as they lift themselves. So how do we help heal what was broken? Yes, there is personal responsibility; we have to strengthen the values of our communities and I believe we also have to move toward it as one people. We have to stop looking at it as "us and them" and start thinking all of it is "us". When we see people stuck in cycles of pain, it's us. When we see people stuck in situations that look hopeless, that's us. How do we lock arms and fix ourselves?

Understanding an individual's unique challenges – outside factors that can limit or even eliminate some choices – can help us as believers and the Body of Christ understand how to better come alongside and support people who face barriers that we don't…without condemnation or judgment.

Imagine a rising generation of advocates with an increased spirit of compassion from the Body of Christ tending to communities in cycles of struggle and pain. The kind of governmental policies from our nation's past, as I have hopefully shown, have served in many ways to diminish African American opportunity and usher people into cycles of poverty and despair. My hope is that an understanding of the past will help us to move towards the pain and despair with compassion and empathy.

Questions for Reflection

1. Why must we address both personal responsibility AND outside circumstances when seeking change and growth for our hurting communities?

2. Why do you think some people neglect personal responsibility when seeking solutions? Conversely, why do some people neglect systems and place all blame on the individual?

3. After reading this section, what are your thoughts about how much a person's backstory might influence their decisions and actions today?

Chapter 10

You Break it, You Buy it

C irca 1952, in Miami, there is a story of a fancy gift shop with all kinds of delicate figurines and fine pottery. The pottery was so exquisite that the shop drew visitors from near and far, some without any intention of making a purchase. People would pick up the pottery and marvel at its color and beauty, admire its craftsmanship. Unfortunately, it became commonplace for people to accidentally mishandle, damage, and break the pottery. The little shop noticed a trend. People would rarely take responsibility for damage they'd caused. After all, they hadn't technically purchased it yet. The store was losing profits when such valuable items would be damaged by seemingly careless customers who were never held accountable.

In response, the store came up with a new policy, one that would quickly be adopted in many other stores. A new sign was proudly placed on the front door: "If you break it, you buy it." This meant the shopper would now be responsible for that which was broken or destroyed. Now in possession of the broken item, they were in charge of the repair, or at least making an attempt to restore the item to the best possible condition.

This later became known as the "Pottery Barn rule". The goal of this policy was to encourage customers to be more careful when handling property that does not belong to them.[60]

This analogy has been used in the political and military arena to suggest that if someone inadvertently creates a problem, that same person is obliged to provide the resources necessary to correct it. Auto insurance policies are often built on this very premise of liability and repair.

When it comes to what we have learned regarding the American experience and the tragedy of what was done to African American people, we know we can't erase the past, but did America do all it could to own it and repair it?

Let's look to answer this by looking at another situation where a nation worked to repair a people it had broken.

Let's Look At the Holocaust

Most people agree that the Jewish Holocaust is one of the most tragic atrocities ever committed against a people group. If you were to talk to any German today, whether they identify as liberal or conservative, most universally agree that the Holocaust sought to steal the dignity, language and identity of free Jewish men and women.

From roughly 1933 to 1945, the Jewish people were stripped of their identities, reduced to mere serial numbers as they were enslaved, brutalized, raped, and treated worse than animals. Under Adolph Hitler's leadership, the German government went on a mission to dehumanize and purge the Jewish people from their sphere of influence. Horribly, the Nazis even referred to those they persecuted as "Lebensunwertes leben", which, roughly translated, means "life unworthy of life."[63,64]

Children in a concentration camp during the Holocaust.
(Galerie Bilderwelt/Getty Images)

After Hitler's regime was shut down, in response, Germany began the arduous process of trying to right some of the wrongs that were committed against the Jewish people. As a part of this effort, in the years since WWII ended, the German nation sought to remove any symbols from the public square that honored Hitler or his regime. Their goal was to eradicate any symbols or other reminders of the Nazi regime that remained in order to prevent further psychological damage to the Jewish people. In fact, if you were to visit Germany today, you would be hard pressed to find a single statue memorializing Hitler or his regime.

Germany then went on a mission to lift up the Jewish people by raising statues of Holocaust victims and they built museums to honor and remember the victims' plight so that humanity would never forget those who were lost. These memorials and museums can be found all over the world, far-reaching beyond the lands in which these atrocities took place.

Continuing in their quest for healing and restitution, in 1952, the German government signed agreements to provide financial payments to Holocaust survivors. As Konrad Adenauer, the Chancellor for West Germany, put it, the payments were an attempt to mitigate the harm done by the "unspeakable crimes committed in the name of the German people" during World War II.[61] It is difficult to estimate the exact amount of money paid by the German government, but in today's terms, Germany says it has distributed over $90 billion in U.S. dollars in the decades since the Holocaust.[62]

This posture continued for decades to attempt to help the Jewish people not be stuck in the plight that they found themselves in when they were delivered from the Holocaust; Germany tried to materially help lift the Jewish people out of the long-term potential generational impact that the Holocaust would otherwise have had. One of the primary goals was to raise the Jewish people up to live in equality with their fellow man. Not just free them and leave them wounded from what they had experienced, but to help aid and heal all that was broken.

Of course, nothing could have ever made it fully right. Lives were lost and destroyed and there was much that could not be undone. The greatest impact resulting from Germany's actions was not just the acknowledgement of the evil wrongs committed, but the efforts made in righting the wrongs done to the Jewish people in order to try to limit additional lingering generational effects.

In Comparison...

In many ways, the Holocaust and the transatlantic slave trade that helped facilitate slavery in America have tragic similarities. While it is true that the majority of slaves were sold into slavery by their own people to white slave traders, it was white slave owners who perpetuated this atrocity for hundreds of years in America. African Americans were stripped of their identities, dehumanized, and enslaved for generations. Families were intentionally broken apart and people were put into forced labor.

Enslaved Persons in the U.S. prior to Emancipation.
(Science History Images/Alamy Stock Photo)

In the midst of this dark hour in our nation, there were many whose consciences were pricked, many who were convicted about the evil being practiced in our nation. Ultimately, a Civil War was fought and won in order to set African Americans free. This was a powerful moment for an enslaved people.

However, when looking closer at the time following Emancipation, there are some distinct differences in the way the United States responded compared to Germany's actions after the Holocaust. The kind of financial aid Germany provided to Jews was not given to newly freed African people, nor were they seen as equal with those who freed them from slavery. In contrast, as mentioned earlier in this book, after approximately twelve years of progress towards equality for black Americans during Reconstruction, what followed was a period of forced segregation and laws that legalized racial inequality for almost a hundred years. Laws made it illegal for African Americans to drink out of the same water fountains, eat at the same restaurants, attend the same schools, participate in the same professional sports leagues, and live in the same neighborhoods as white people. Also as mentioned earlier, thousands of monuments for confederate soldiers were constructed all over the nation to memorialize the South's participation in the Civil War, and for the vast majority of African Americans, they made it impossible for them to forget their time in bondage. The overall message to people of color in this country during that time seemed to be "You are free, but you are not equal."

I wonder how the lives of people of color descended from slavery would be different today had the United States had a similar response to that of Germany's to the Holocaust. Of course, the atrocities of the Holocaust endured for a much shorter period of time as compared to American slavery, and

Holocaust survivors would have had some ability to reconnect with family and friends afterwards for help and support, but they also didn't have to see their former oppressors glorified with statuary and other memorials, either. They were even given meaningful financial support to help them get back on their feet. During Reconstruction, America *did* make a start at helping right some of the wrongs of slavery immediately after the Civil War ended (including financial support), but that help was, unfortunately, short-lived. Today's welfare system is an attempt to help people in need, including those whose families were unable to build legacy wealth over the years, but it seems that, no matter what side of the political aisle you're on, most people would agree that the system is riddled with problems which we as a country have not been able to resolve to this day.

As a result, the journey of the African American community since slavery has been a uniquely difficult and long struggle to rise up. In fact, African Americans today still disproportionately represent the largest demographic in poverty among every racial group in the United States.[63]

Most everyone agrees that slavery was wrong, but is it possible that a person of color might look at Germany's handling of the years after the Holocaust and feel that America doesn't quite get HOW wrong slavery was? Or that our nation really isn't invested in fixing some of the legacy effects of slavery and the ensuing era of segregation? I'll leave that for you to ponder.

Questions for Reflection

1. What in your eyes was the biggest difference between how Germany and the U.S. responded to their past crimes against humanity?

2. What impact do you think those differences might have had on the outcomes of individual survivors in both cases?

3. What Scriptures can you think of that speak to making amends and acknowledging wrongdoing as a people group?

Chapter 11

The Outliers

Have you ever felt the gravitational pull of peer pressure urging you to get on board with an idea? Maybe some fad, trend, or the latest idea at work is beckoning you to buy-in. Maybe you're even unsettled with the idea, but since everyone else is doing it, you quickly jump on board. This often happens in our daily lives, and it can be fine sometimes to just go along when not much is at stake; I mean, who cares what toothpaste you pick for the house really? But what happens when the idea presented is something big, something very wrong that your conscience can't align with? What do we do then? The truth is, it takes courage to stand amid the gravitational pull of the crowd and dare to be different. It's hard to be an outlier.

Many men and women have done this at crucial times in history when an outlier who told the crowd "no" was needed, because sometimes what you'll find in history is that the crowd is wrong and a champion needs to rise up.

One man appears to do this in a famous photo taken in 1936. It shows a crowd of people saluting Hitler as far as the eyes can see. Still, if you look closely, there is a needle in a haystack amid the crowd as one man refused to raise his hand in salute.

In a sea of people saluting what was clearly wrong, one man folded his arms and said, "no more." For years no one knew who this man was and what his reasons may have been.

But in 1991, a woman named Irene Eckler identified the man as her father, August Landmesser, a worker at the Blohm + Voss shipyard in Hamburg, Germany (while another family has come forward claiming the man in the picture is someone else entirely, the more popular view accepts the Landmesser identification).[64]

As we learn more about his story, we find out that Landmesser had reasons to resist saluting.

Man indicated by circle is believed to be August Landmesser, 1936.

Landmesser's descendants maintain that August was a member of the Nazi Party from 1931 to 1935, but that his party membership came to an abrupt end after he married Irma Eckler – a Jewish woman.[65]

The whole story we will never know, but we do know that one fate-filled day amid the gravitational pull of the crowd, he did the right thing and said "no". He was an outlier.

History holds many stories of such outliers. When we flip back through the pages of our country's history, we find the truths of some incredible men and women who used their voices, their resources, and their platforms to create change and forge new paths in challenging cultural climates. We love a good story of an outlier, or an underdog who rises up against incredible odds. And then, often lesser known, are outliers among the outliers.

There is the story of an American duo; two men who chose the road less traveled: The Tappan brothers.

Arthur and Lewis Tappan were young boys growing up in Massachusetts in the early 1800s during The Second Great Awakening, a time when the Gospel was boldly preached and people were convicted to develop a personal relationship with God; a time when calls for social reform took root. A time when slavery was still legal in the U.S.

The Tappan brothers would amass incredible wealth as silk merchants and through the establishment of America's first commercial credit-rating service. However, it was what the Tappan boys would do with their wealth that would be considered revolutionary in their day.

In 1832, Lewis Tappan rented and renovated a 2400 seat theater in New York City to provide a place for Charles Grandison Finney to preach the Gospel. Here, at the Chatham Street Chapel,

Finney preached to a multi-racial church and would denounce slavery from the pulpit, refusing communion to slave owners and traders. The Tappans pushed for Finney to eliminate "The Black Pew" and to abolish separate seating so that African Americans would be fully integrated into the predominantly white society as equals. The brothers lobbied for placing an African American man on the board of trustees. Why did they do this?

Because even more radical than the abolitionists fighting against slavery, the Tappans were fighting for equality. They believed that African Americans were their equals in the eyes of God and society. They believed in and demanded "universal liberty" for all people.

The powerful Tappans would establish America's first Anti-Slavery society where Arthur would serve as President. They distributed pamphlets through the mail. They provided the financial backing for the establishment of Oberlin College; one of the first to admit African Americans and the first to admit women to learn alongside white men, at a time where no one was calling for it. They financed the legal defense for the Africans who mutinied aboard the Amistad, and once released, arranged for their tutoring to learn English. They funded the Underground Railroad and they created anti-slavery pamphlets that they distributed all through the South.

Their efforts did not go unchallenged by the mainstream majority culture. Mobs attacked Lewis' home, dragging his furniture into the street and setting it ablaze. Arthur's store was attacked and his effigy was publicly burned. Even the newly-elected President Andrew Jackson would be angered and demand censorship of their distributed writings, leading to mobs descending on post offices to seize and burn the bags of pamphlets. Still, they pressed forward in pursuit of creating a culture of equality through universal education and activism.[66]

What do the Tappan brothers teach us about being an effective outlier? They made an internal decision and expressed it with outward action. In a sense, they were prophetic and understood the needs of the day and took risks and used available resources to elevate an oppressed people whom they viewed as equal in their very created nature. They demonstrated that they feared God more than they feared man, and their actions created inroads of opportunity for African Americans that was culturally way before their time. It's reasonable to assume that they didn't fear the elevation of African Americans to be a threat, but a welcome progress for the improvement of the country as a whole. What if more people had stepped in, joined forces, and continued the trajectory? What could have been?

God loves to appoint and empower outliers: Moses, David, Ruth, Elijah, John the Baptist, Paul, the Tappan brothers, and maybe even *you*. In many ways, as a believer, you are already an outlier in this world. How will the Holy Spirit nudge you to serve as a conduit of his love and to be an outlier among outliers? There will be great temptation to shrink back and move with the crowd, but at crucial times we need outliers.

Questions for Reflection

1. Can you think of any other outlier stories in Scripture that bring insight to God's desire for unity and harmony for His children?

2. How did the Tappan brothers demonstrate they were after more than just emancipation?

3. Have you ever had to stand alone when fighting for something? What was the result?

4. Take a quiet moment and ask the Lord where he may want you to stand as an outlier in your own spheres.

Chapter 12

Where Are You?

Over the last decade, the electrical systems in our cars have gotten a major upgrade. Gone are the days of one gauge for gas and one for speed. You can scroll through an extensive digital maintenance list and find information on your exact tire pressure, your washer fluid, your oil level, and what temperature your kids are blasting the rear AC to. There are safety alarms to let you know when your door is open or when someone is driving in your blind spot. It's like the car is continuously running a self-assessment so you have the most up-to-date information. This is so helpful to minimize surprises! No one likes to run out of gas or find themselves in need of an emergency oil change.

This applies to our lives, too. We complete all kinds of preventative and diagnostic assessments. We do financial check-ups, annual health and dental check-ups, and, as part of the home-buying process, we do an inspection to check the integrity of the property.

But how often do we check the gauges of our attitudes and desires? Similar to our cars, taking a personal inventory can shed light on what's going on beneath the surface. It can help us identify something that may not be functioning optimally, or that may be preventing growth. Maybe you have plenty of gas in the tank, but your oil level is low. Maybe your battery is fully juiced but your windshield wiper fluid is below the recommended level. Gauges bring awareness that leads to action.

In many ways this mirrors our walk with God. There are places in our lives where we could be thriving and walking closely with God and places where we need to seek more growth. However, we're unlikely to seek growth if we don't know what's lacking. Gauges can be helpful in revealing where we stand.

The Psalmist in 139 was asking for the Lord to gauge him:

Psalm 139:23-24 (NIV)

²³ Search me, God, and know my heart; test me and know my anxious thoughts.

²⁴ See if there is any offensive way in me, and lead me in the way everlasting.

In the pursuit of growing in the area of oneness and walking in kingdom unity, I recommend doing an intentional checking of gauges. Assessment and diagnosis is essential for effective treatment and fine-tuning operations.

So I ask: How are you doing? How is the Church doing?

This book has now spent time talking about the challenges that arise relating to our racial unity. It's clear that there are factions of people who have wildly differing beliefs and views on the solutions. Of course, these differences occur among our various political parties, but they can occur even *within* a particular party. Sometimes you'll see differences reflected regionally, or even within a single family unit. But what about your own personal condition? We each show up to the conversation with different exposures and experiences. Perhaps you've been exposed in this book to some things you've never thought of or known about.

In order to create a kind of "gauge" with which to measure your own perspective on issues of race in America, with much prayer and after many conversations on the topic across a widely diverse spectrum of peoples, I've designed "The Oneness Continuum".

It illustrates the various places we can find ourselves in the spectrum of this journey. I highly encourage you to read through it in its entirety and find yourself in it. Your authentic self. It's important that you don't put yourself where you aren't, or where you wish to be. This is not meant to be a pegboard to invoke any sense of shame. You may identify with qualities across the continuum. If we are going to move toward one another and those with different views, we have to be honest about where we currently sit in our understanding of and role in the conversation about race in this country. In this honest place, we can meet each other exactly where we are.

The Oneness Continuum: Unengaged > Emerging > Aware > Equipped > Advocating

Someone who is what we would term **Unengaged** might make a self-assessment that sounds something like this: '*I try my best to do what's right and to treat people with kindness, dignity and respect no matter who they are. As a result, my life has* *been generally unaffected by the major tensions of race and racism that pop up so frequently in the media. While some of the things I see occasionally can be troubling, they're so far from my personal sphere and upbringing that none of it has led me to a personal desire for study of the issues being raised. I know that personally I've done nothing wrong in my own life to contribute to any of the disunity. Therefore, I sense no significant need to engage or search my own soul any further on this topic. I live my life respectfully and believe that much of the issues we see are caused by fringe groups and bad apples on both sides of the aisle and not every-day good people. My perspective is relatively fixed. All my core group of friends look like me, think like me and we generally all agree on all these major issues. Conversations on this topic with those who aren't like me rarely have ever happened in my life and I have yet to be inspired personally to seek them out beyond what perhaps my workplace or place of worship has required me to do.'*

Someone who is **Emerging** might say: '*I don't fully understand what's going on in our world in regard to culture and race, but I sense that something is really wrong. I have tried my best to treat people as equals but the chorus of discontent and the situation in the world around me regarding culture and race can no longer be ignored. I sense that there are things around me that I don't fully understand, but I fear engaging or saying anything as I don't want to be labeled, judged, or called out for misunderstanding. That being said, these fears have not kept me completely silent, and this has led me to seek further counsel from close friends or confidants. I don't know where this journey will take me, but I'm slowly becoming more open to the idea that perhaps there is a lot that I don't understand.'*

Someone fitting in the **Aware** category might say: '*There has been an "aha" moment in my life that has challenged all previous* *understanding that I have had on this issue. I am keenly aware that something is wrong and so now I humbly submit myself to guidance and seek greater understanding. As I sit under others and learn, I discover that there are core foundations of understanding theologically, ecclesiastically, historically, nationally, and relationally all around me that I was unaware of. As a result, I've been challenged in my heart to humbly begin a deeper journey towards truth and understanding. I am now open to hearing from others' experiences and perspectives, seeking the change needed to grow. Something is wrong in our world and even in the Church and I realize that we can't stay the same. I also realize that for change to take place in our world, it starts with me. I want to change.'*

The **Equipped** might say something like this: *'I have learned and grown over a period of time, and I now desire passionately to go to the next level of understanding. This desire is marked by a distinct transition from solely relying on diversity-related reading assignments from my workplace, school, or church to beginning my own relentless self-initiated search for truth. I have passionately and on my own begun to read, study, research, and ingest material written by minorities and other advocates on this subject. While I may not agree with all of what I read, I am constantly seeking to understand more about myself and the perspectives of others in order to grow. This growth is not merely for the sake of gaining more knowledge, but in order to be better equipped to have organic conversations with my friends, family, community, and those around me. I am initiating conversations with those close to me and those who are not like me. My desire is to move from being a student to becoming a vocal advocate for racial reconciliation. I am self-initiated on this issue.'*

An **Advocate** might say: *'I feel the call of Jesus to go out into "all nations" and to make disciples, with a renewed understanding* *of and focus on the message of oneness and reconciliation of all people. I recognize that "all nations" doesn't necessarily require that I get on an airplane and go elsewhere but it surely requires that I now go to my neighbor on the other side of the street or maybe even in the church pew. I believe that there are systemic relational issues in our culture that can only be healed by moving toward one another in loving relationships. I also believe that each person is made in the image of God and worthy of being treated with dignity and respect no matter what their ethnic or cultural background is. I seek opportunities to build bridges in my personal life and to grow as a conversationalist as this message burns in my core. I have begun to engage in new deep relationships with people around me and I have begun to teach and lead others. I share my personal story openly and honestly without shame as a part of the healing process. My desire is not just to inspire change in other people but to practically inspire catalytic change in the organizations that I am a part of. I am actively building into and creating other advocates. People see me as a leader on this subject and my desire is to raise up the same.'*

So where do you find yourself? You may be realizing at this point that there is a lot more going on than you originally understood, but find yourself at a loss to know where to even begin to make a change – in yourself and in the world. In the next few final chapters, I'll cast some vision to help inspire you to discover the possibilities waiting right around the corner.

Questions for Reflection:

1. Based on where you find yourself, what's one step you could take to continue the growth process?

2. Where do you think you were on the continuum when you began the book?

3. Where do you think your church is on the continuum?

Chapter 13

Share Your News Story

I n this present day of non-stop 24 hours a day cycles of news it can be hard to escape the constant chatter and barrage of the media. News agencies get criticized a lot, and they can be annoying, but for all their shortcomings, they actually *do* serve an invaluable purpose.

News agencies invite us into worlds that we would otherwise be unaware of. Our own vantage point is limited, but news agencies expand our perspective. A person who is living in San Diego, California would not know what a person living in Baltimore, Maryland is going through without the news. A person living in America would not know what is happening in Afghanistan without the news. The news gives us the opportunity to be aware and to care. This happens on citywide and statewide levels as well. Without the news, we would be unaware and therefore have no opportunity to care for or consider anyone outside our own immediate spheres, because our vantage point is limited.

News agencies keep us from becoming insulated in our own life's circumstances and help connect us to a bigger picture – one that connects us to each other's humanity.

Inside every one of us is a personal "news story". Each one of us has a personal experience with race in America and within the Church. This is our "Race Narrative": our personal story of what we've been taught about race, what we have come to believe, and our lived experiences. A Race Narrative is a tool that can be utilized to increase our own insight into our experiences and how they have shaped us, to help us be understood by others, and to increase our own understanding of another's experience.

When a small group of people of different backgrounds, cultures, races, and perspectives gather to share their Race Narratives, the conversations elicited may not always be easy, but the members will learn so much from listening to one another, and significant growth can be an outcome. Each individual narrative gives us new collective eyes into each other's worlds. Even if you do not have the opportunity to share your personal race narrative right away, the process of writing and reflecting on it will be enlightening.

For small groups of people wanting to engage in sharing Race Narratives with one another, it is essential to have a highly confidential and respect-filled environment where everyone listens to the stories shared without criticism or judgment. It is best to keep the group size small, perhaps no more than 6 people; people you are doing life with – your friends, family, or a Bible study group.

Here are some useful tips and thought-provoking questions that can get you started in writing your own personal Race Narrative.

Race Narrative–Your Unique Experience with Issues of Race

Your race narrative is the unique story of your upbringing and introduction into the concept and experience of race. Race exists as a major concept in our world, and our vantage points and experiences are often very different. Putting together your narrative can often yield surprises, even to you! Be prepared to discover how the ups, the downs, the good, the bad, and the ugly all shaped you. Typically, 20 minutes allows enough time to share the relevant chapters in each person's story.

Provided below is a list of questions which I invite you to prayerfully engage with as you process your story. Remember, there is no condemnation here. Your story is your story; we are all products of the environments and events we experienced growing up on this planet. As much as possible, try not to edit yourself for fear of being judged. It is recommended that you consider writing your journey out to help your process, which often makes it much easier to share within a group.

Questions for consideration while creating your "Race Narrative:

1. What was your first memory of being aware of the concept of race? Describe that experience. What did it teach you (include both good and bad)?

2. What lessons were you taught as a child by your family (including extended family) regarding culture and race?

3. What words were used to describe other people groups and minorities?

4. What overt and subtle messages did you receive from your immediate and extended family?

5. Who did you hang out with as a child growing up? What were your schools and neighborhoods like in terms of cultural diversity?

6. What did the experiences you had in those environments teach you about race?

7. Did you encounter other ethnic groups when growing up? What were those experiences like?

8. What were you taught about dating relationships between races?

9. What moments in your past involving race stand out to you as either positive or negative? Describe how these events affected you.

Note: Most people are unaware of this part of their life's story. We tend to move through childhood into adolescence through various experiences without considering how they shaped us. You will perhaps remember things you forgot about completely. So please take the time to be prayerful, reflective, and painstakingly honest with yourself about your upbringing as you prepare to share. These stories are crucial because they have shaped who we are not just as individuals, but as a community. Our stories each belong to history and our history with one another. This process will be filled with deep discovery, triumph, regrets and maybe even tears, but it yields tremendous fruit in each person's journey towards oneness and understanding.

My hope is that as you share your story in your group, you are able to connect to one another relationally and to each other's humanity.

Tell your story, because there is power in it!

Revelation 12:11 (NIV)

[11] "They triumphed over him by the blood of the Lamb and by the word of their testimony; they did not love their lives so much as to shrink from death."

To put this practice into play, a good friend of mine, Michele, shares her race narrative below. My hope is that it inspires your own story. We are all on a journey toward oneness.

"I was born in 1967 in Baltimore at St. Agnes Hospital. My parents lived off of Patapsco Avenue. When I was one and a half, my family moved to Reading, PA. I learned only months ago that one of the biggest reasons for this was the riots that occurred in Baltimore in 1968 after Martin Luther King, Jr. was assassinated. The riots scared my parents, both in their early 20's, enough so that they literally fled.

"So I grew up white in a predominantly white agricultural community outside of Reading. There were no people of color in my entire Kindergarten through 12th grade school experience. I saw them on TV when I watched Sesame Street, or the Love Boat (gotta love Isaac), and later, the Cosby Show. I have no memories of my parents or friends ever talking about race, although my mom's dad never had good things to say about any of the Hispanic people that were relocating to Reading in search of work. As far as schooling went, I learned the typical 1970's curriculum about slavery and the Civil War, but that was the extent of my education on race relations.

"It wasn't until 1986, when I moved into my dorm my sophomore year at Penn State, that I made my first black friend. She was in the room next to mine, and we shared so many interests–film, art, music, boys...she was there for me when my heart got broken and to stay up all hours talking about the mysteries of life. We didn't talk about race issues much, although she did tease me playfully every time I brushed my "white girl hair" over my shoulder.

"I entered adulthood believing that racism was bad, that the "n" word was the worst word you could ever say, and that I should treat everyone with kindness and respect, regardless of their skin color. I believed that civil rights issues had been hashed out in the sixties, and we were now living in a post-racist America. I had black friends, so I passed the test as being "not racist or prejudiced" in my mind.

"I moved back to Baltimore in 1995. Over the years, I have made many more friends, some of them black. I became heavily involved in Habitat for Humanity in an impoverished neighborhood called Sandtown and began forming friendships and relationships with folks in that neck of town...I grew to love the neighborhood and everyone in it. I saw first-hand the struggle it can be to just own a decent house and an acceptable standard of living...even if you're doing all the "right" things. I read The Corner and watched "The Wire" and found my compassion for the plight of people living in the inner city struggling with drugs, crime, poverty and hopelessness growing and growing.

"All this to say, I felt pretty good about myself and my "non-racist/non-prejudiced" status by the time Freddie Gray became a household name. Surely I wasn't part of the problem.

"And yet, I was.

"Looking back at some of the things I have said and done that have harmed people of color, it is hard for me to believe I didn't see it then. Most often, the harm was done by my silence... standing mute while white people around me said overtly racist things. I never had the courage to speak up. But there are two events that stand out where I WISH all I had done was hold my tongue.

"The first was in the late nineties. I had a close friend at work who is black. We did lunch together, we played crazy practical jokes together, we laughed, we cried, we had FUN together.

"Our friendship was several years old when it happened. I met a guy on an online dating site and fell in love. I literally walked around with my head in the clouds for the next four months. But my friend had met him and had some concerns about him. She pulled me aside one day and warned me to guard my heart...to keep my head and make sure this guy was everything he said he was before doing something crazy like running off and marrying him.

"How DARE she imply that my man might not be trust-worthy? I said "Maybe in YOUR culture that's how men are, but not in MINE."

"It is a testament to my friend that she is still my friend. I knew the moment the words were out of my mouth how terrible they were. "Where did that even COME from?" I asked myself, but the damage was done. That's where my brain went in its indignation and anger...straight to attacking her culture. And our friendship was severely broken for a long time after that. Certainly no amount of me saying I was sorry was ever going to unsay those words. But as I alluded to above, thankfully my friend had enough grace and mercy for both of us, and eventually she accepted my apology and allowed me to attempt to repair our friendship.

"The second example is much worse.

"Several years ago, a black family moved into the townhome two doors down from me...a single working mother with kids. I live in a predominantly white townhome community north of Baltimore, so I can imagine now that it must have been a little intimidating moving into my neighborhood as a person of color, not knowing what to expect from the neighbors.

"Turns out what to expect was us white neighbors getting our noses out of joint every time this new family didn't abide by our HOA rules, or left their toys all over the sidewalk, or failed to shovel their snow in a timely manner (horrors!), or talked too loud, or had cars stopping by at all hours of the night. My older neighbors and I started talking amongst ourselves... something had to be done. The straw that broke the camel's back was a fight that broke out one night right in front of the new family's house. A number of black teens were attacking another black teen. 9-1-1 was called, but everyone had fled before police arrived.

"After that, I and one other neighbor wrote to the owner of the house the new family lived in (their landlord) and spelled out all of our grievances. No way were we going to tolerate having the "inner city culture" brought onto our peaceful street. The landlord evicted the family not long after.

"I helped get a hard-working black single mom and her kids kicked out of their home because they didn't fit in with my idea of what a neighbor should be. That is the naked truth of it. Worse, in my mind, I still wasn't racist or prejudiced. I was just being a good citizen.

"And this is what I believed all these years...right up until a cop kneeled on a black man's neck during an arrest, at the very least contributing to, if not wholly causing, the black man's death. The black man's name was George Floyd.

"I watched the rioting that came after in horror, tears streaming down my face. My Facebook feed was filled with my white liberal friends telling me I was racist if I wasn't speaking out about racism. Telling me I WAS part of the problem if I wasn't educating myself, watching this documentary, following that podcast, reading this book.

"The tears turned into anger. How DARE people accuse ME of being racist???? Did they know about all my black friends? I was positive this was all some liberal agenda to make me hate my country, but that it would all die down soon. My black friends weren't even bringing up George Floyd with me...they must not have been that upset! What was the big deal?

"I shut Facebook off for three days. I stopped watching the news. If I just ignored it, it would all go away, right?

"But then a thought came to me. I believe it was God in my heart whispering "What would you stand to lose by asking your black friends how they are experiencing the events in the U.S. right now? What would be the downside of reading a book written by a black person about racial issues? How much would it hurt to just *listen?*"

"I've been doing my best to listen ever since. And I have gained so much...learned so much...that has completely changed the way I view racial relations. I have made new friends, strengthened existing friendships, and become engaged in the conversation in a whole new way that feels life affirming and healing. I still have a lot to learn and experience, but I am so thankful that God gave me a chance to grow in this area this side of Heaven."

Questions for Reflection:

1. What emotions bubbled up as you read Michele's personal narrative?

2. What value is there in sharing our personal narratives on race?

3. What barriers or fears do you have when entertaining the idea of pondering or sharing your own story?

Chapter 14

Seeing one another

As evocative as Michele's story is, a familiar thread is revealed: one of the primary barriers to oneness is that we don't have the eyes to really see one another. One of the tremendous opportunities I believe the Church has in being a part of the vision toward healing the racial divide is to reclaim the Biblical beauty of oneness that we see reflected continuously in the Scriptures. Paying closer attention to the true beauty in the diversity we find in the pages of Scripture may just help to focus our eyes on the beauty of all the image-bearers around us.

Scripture highlights so much color and culture through its pages and these depictions bring dignity and representation to each of us, no matter what our skin color is. Taking the time to pause and depict these unique ethnicities and skin colors is one way to bring unity and healing as we seek to experience more of the vision for oneness the Bible proclaims.

In Chapter 1, we learned how the Bible often paints a diverse tapestry to reflect the cultural barrier-breaking posture of the Gospel that occurred in the book of Acts, where people from many nations became one in Christ. Sometimes the diverse depiction is there just to show the significance that a certain unique culture played in the history of our faith. The stories and settings of the Bible are much more colorful than we typically imagine.

Often, we can miss this colorful Biblical beauty because of the ethnocentric approach of how the Gospel arrived on our shores. I believe that with a little re-focusing of our Biblical lenses, we can regain the fullness which was intended as the Bible came into being.

Here is an example of diverse beauty you may have missed – and it's a big one:

Considering all the movies and picture story-books we have seen about the life of Moses, it's interesting that we never hear much about his wife, Zipporah, including her key traits.

Numbers 12:1 KJV

[1] *"And Miriam and Aaron spake against Moses because of the Ethiopian woman whom he had married: for he had married an Ethiopian woman."*

There is a lot going on in this passage regarding an argument that took place among Miriam, Aaron and Moses, but for the intent of this conversation I would like to highlight what's sitting on the surface and revealed in this exchange about Moses' wife.

Zipporah was from Ethiopia! Many translations say Cyrene, which is the same thing. As an Ethiopian, she would have been a dark-skinned woman from the continent of Africa. The word Ethiopia comes from the Greek meaning "burnt faces".[67]

Why is this news to us? Also, why has Zipporah been left out of so many opportunities to be depicted in art and movies? She's relatively invisible to Bible readers of today.

Perhaps one reason is that Moses has been so often depicted to resemble the Europeans who would have been the intended audience for the art being created hundreds of years ago. As movies came into being, casting Zipporah authentically as a black woman did not fit the prevailing picture which the movie-makers (primarily European descendants) had in mind when they thought about the Moses account – cinematically or otherwise. Certainly some omissions of traits and heritage can be innocent, but when one distortion prevails and becomes the dominant image, it can feel intentional. For people looking to see the Bible in full color, the omission of Zipporah's true ethnicity and her lack of depiction is tragic.

Zipporah is not the only key figure we haven't fully seen because of our historically narrow approach. This approach robs us of all of the beautiful diversity God has painted for us throughout Scripture.

In the book of Acts, we read of another story painted with such rich colors: the Ethiopian eunuch. He was a court official for Candace, the Queen of the Ethiopians, and in charge of all her treasures. He had been traveling home from Jerusalem and encountered a divine appointment with Philip, orchestrated by the Holy Spirit.

Here we have two men, a Syrian evangelist and an African man of great authority and distinction, sitting together in a chariot, having a Bible study. An African man would forever be memorialized in Scripture as the first non-Jewish believer to be baptized into the faith. God demonstrates his pursuit of the Ethiopian's heart by sending an angel to Philip the evangelist with specific instructions to seek him out. This results in a conversion, a baptism, and a miracle of Philip being swept away by the spirit of the Lord once his God-appointed mission was completed.

None of us can undo the past, but we can strive toward a fuller reflection of what we see in Scripture for our future. What if we could highlight the beautiful diversity we read of in the Bible as we preach, teach, exhort, lead small groups, and do devotionals?

What if the diverse beauty found throughout the Bible could be reflected in the artwork of the Church? Of course, I am not saying that every conversation needs to be about race and culture, but I am suggesting that we seek a moment at times to stop and notice the locations and backgrounds of some of the people and places we often gloss over as we read the Scriptures. You may find it quite surprising how constantly colorful the Bible is.

I believe this is part of what will help us overcome some of the problematic ethnocentric narratives that we inherited from the Europeans that brought the Bible to the shores of America. This historically-influenced approach to the Bible has caused us to look at the Scriptures in a way often devoid of authentic cultural representation. This mindset was adopted, either consciously or subconsciously, and decades of monochrome cinematic and other artistic depictions of Biblical persons have eroded most of our colorful visual framework when we read the Scriptures. Think of how reclaiming a full-color picture of Biblical beauty would be beneficial for all who hold its pages!

There are countless examples of how the Bible brings a much fuller and diverse picture of humanity that we miss. I believe that Scripture is painted with color so that each one of us can see ourselves. I believe that if we pause for a moment as we read the Scriptures and just authentically highlight the people, places, and the uniqueness of the people God uses, we will truly begin to see each other in a new way and recognize the image bearing nature he placed in each of us.

Questions for Reflection:

1. Can you think of any familiar artwork, movies, or picture books that contain an inaccurate depiction?

2. How does seeking true representation in art and media foster unity?

3. Think of a few of your favorite people in the Bible and do some digging into where they were from and any societal implications they may have faced in their culture. How does this expand your insight into the story?

Chapter 15

Final Charge

I
t is my utmost desire that the words across these pages have
enlightened, encouraged, challenged, and fueled a passion
for authentic unity within you. The call to oneness is not just
a personal desire but one that emanates from the very heart of
God for all of His children. As a pastor, I cannot help but to
make a few final charges as you follow the Lord's leading as a
result of the information and revelation you have ingested. Be a
bridge builder who sacrifices for the sake of what Jesus calls us
to and who He calls us to be. This work will take an abundance
of courage, grace, mercy and patience as we move toward one
another in important dialogue and the way we approach one
another will be key.

Be An Effective Bridge Builder

Cooking shows have taken the world by storm. We have
baking contests, kid cooking shows, professional chef battles,
how-to-cook tutorials and even an entire Food Network! We
have a national fascination with them. In a timed competition

show, it is essential that the chef leaves enough time for the proper presentation of their created dish. Professional chefs and amateur home chefs alike understand that the presentation of the dish matters just as much as the taste of the food! We taste the food with our eyes before it ever touches our tongue. The taste of the food doesn't matter if it doesn't look good enough to eat. Is the sauce drizzled just right? Does the garnish accentuate the dish? Are the items arranged in an artful way?

Two restaurants may have an entree consisting of the same ingredients: the same meat, potatoes and vegetables. The nutritional value and volume of food is the same. However, one appears to be thrown onto the plate and the other is thoughtfully arranged with care and precision. Which one are you more excited to experience? Which restaurant are you more likely to return to, and bring your friends?

Whether we like it or not, the same is true in the conversation on culture and race. Part of the reason that we aren't receiving from one another is because of how the information is being presented. Do we have respect, care, and concern for one another as we communicate, or are we just slopping things on a plate and saying: "Eat it!"?

People are more likely to receive something plated with care and respect.

The Bible says Jesus was full of grace AND truth. He had both. The way we communicate with one another matters. Truth, without grace, isn't received. Grace, without truth, is a lie.

As we move toward one another, care, respect, love, and grace are going to be crucial elements of the plate if we want to truly hear from one another. This isn't about coming to agreement in a moment's notice, but creating an environment where we can have real discussion. It will be uncomfortable at times to have these conversations, but in an environment where there is trust, respect and care, difficult conversations can happen, and unity can be fostered.

Sacrifice For One Another

As believers, we also follow Jesus into His sacrifice. Jesus tells us over and over to count the cost, take up our cross in order to follow Him. This may be one of the hardest things He asks us to do: dying to self. I'm not suggesting you cast aside your values or your Biblical convictions, but I am suggesting that you move towards others *because* of them. How do we move towards one another in Christ-likeness?

When my wife Christine and I got married, we quickly realized that we came from different backgrounds in terms of how the air conditioner temperatures were set in our respective childhood homes. Christine came from a background where her family loved to have the temperature in the house set at a chilly 68°. I came from a background where my family enjoyed a toasty 77°.

When Christine and I started to regulate the thermostat in our first home together, we quickly realized that we had a significant gap in our experiences and preferences. I would push the temperature up, and when I wasn't looking, Christine would push it down and the cycle would continue over and over. It was cute at first, but then tension started to build. Christine thought it was too hot and I thought it was too cold, so we knew we had to find a way to move forward that we both could embrace. Together, we decided that in order to move forward we could not stay in our pre-fixed places. We both had to sacrifice.

After a lot of conversation and prayer, I am pleased to announce that our house is now set to 72 degrees. We each moved a few degrees towards one another. It was uncomfortable for both of us at first, but soon it was unnoticeable and the mutual sacrifice for the benefit of each other increased our love for each other. In the end, we got something better; we discovered our temperature preferences actually changed and adapted! When our sons marry, they will take their learned experience of 72 degrees and find a new way with their own spouses!

What are you willing to give up in order to move toward others? Where are you willing to be uncomfortable in order to follow Jesus into this calling of sacrifice? What are you willing to give up to experience God's vision? I believe that the Church is the only answer to the division and strife that we see today in our world.

As you read these final words, you've likely consumed a new mass of information and experienced the gamut of emotions. Taking an honest look into the origins of our race relations and considering your own personal race narrative is not for the faint of heart. I commend you for your persistence. As valuable as returning to Episode One and shedding light on our current societal struggles can be, there is no point if all you have amassed is facts and information. The pages of Scripture don't exist for the aim of information. The point is, and has always been, transformation. Christ came to transform the world, your continent, your country, your town, your church, you.

I bless you in the name of Jesus to have eyes to see the beauty and image-bearing nature of your neighbor, a sharp mind to identify places and people in need of healing, a heart overflowing with love and compassion and hands and feet to build bridges of unity and oneness where He leads you. I commission you as a royal priesthood, being rooted and established in Christ's love which surpasses all knowledge to be an agent of healing and reconciliation in the spheres He places you in.

Now that we know "What's Goin On", let us see more clearly, love more intentionally, and reap the rewards of oneness.

Questions for Reflection:

1. Make a quick bullet point inventory of the new things you've learned. How will it be useful in your quest to be an agent of unity in your personal spheres?

2. Were you able to identify any barriers keeping you from pursuing the type of unity God desires for us to experience?

3. Consider where God may want to use you as a bridge builder or places He may be asking you to sacrifice in order to promote unity.

4. What is next for you? What topics piqued your curiosity and beckon you to dig deeper in discovering how God can use you to bring His unity on Earth, as it is in heaven?

Further Reading

Below are a few of the materials that helped shape Michele and I as we sought to understand the myriad factors affecting racial issues in America today. We encourage you to read them for yourself as you continue your own journey.

Building a Multiethnic Church: A Gospel Vision of Love, Grace, and Reconciliation in a Divided World by Derwin L. Gray and Matt Chandler. Published by Thomas Nelson (2021).

Compassion (&) Conviction: The AND Campaign's Guide to Faithful Civic Engagement by Justin Giboney, Michael Wear, and Chris Butler. Published by IVP (2020).

Oneness Embraced: Reconciliation, The Kingdom, and How We Are Stronger Together by Tony Evans. Published by Moody Publishers (2011).

Under Our Skin: Getting Real About Race. Getting Free from the Fears and Frustrations that Divide Us by Benjamin Watson. Published by Tyndale Momentum (2015).

Acknowledgements

K hori would like to thank the following individuals and organizations for their support for this project: My mother Dr. Vondelear Smith-Hill, Khamari Smith, Tresean Gore, Johnny Shelton, Matt Stover, Danny O'Brien, Beaulah Lokeman, Harold & Jeanne Padgett, Dr. Cain Hope-Felder, Shea Strickland, Luke Casagrande, Barry Elliott, Ben Abell, Frank Kelly, Brian Kelly, John Kelly, David Kelly, Dave Yacoub, John Terry, Nate Lomax, Grace Fellowship Church, and countless others. I am eternally grateful for all those who have shaped my personal story and understanding of race and race-related issues. I will forever cherish the hours of conversations, your insights, and the ways you have walked alongside me. Thank you to the many people who have provided a listening ear and sage wisdom as I embarked on the process of writing these words. I couldn't have done it without you. I thank those who took the time to read early versions of this manuscript and for the thoughtful, grace-filled feedback you provided. This book is better than I could have written on my own because of *you*. To the many people who not only gave of their time, but also their financial resources to support the printing of this book, I am indebted to you in more than just a financial way. Your belief in this project helped me press forward when it might've been easier to quit. Finally, I could have never done this without the loving support (both moral and tangible) of my family – my loving wife Christine, who spent hours reading and polishing my words. To my two beautiful sons, Kamden and Kellen: I hope this book helps make the world a better place for you as you grow into men. May you be bridge builders and bridge crossers for the glory of the One in whose image you were created. Above all, I thank my greatest teacher, my Lord and Creator Jesus Christ for choosing to use me of all people to spread this message of reconciliation. All glory to God, who is above all.

In addition to the above, Michele would like to thank those who have shaped her journey…people who have showed her unconditional grace and patience in the face of her lack of knowledge surrounding issues of race…you know who you are, but I'll call out some of you here: Michelle McCallum, Allen McCallum, Keysha DuBose, Paul Durazzo, and Ebony Hines. Thank you for giving me a chance to understand and for your mercy when I have failed you. To my mom and dad, who encouraged me to work on this project with Khori and spent hours talking about our work, thank you…your love and willingness to enter into this conversation is one of God's most precious gifts to me. To my two sisters, one biological (Deborah Reber), one spiritual (Kelly Feehely), who have walked beside me this entire time and were the first to encourage me to try to understand the experiences of people who don't look like me, thanks just isn't enough. Deb, an accomplished author in her own right, was my literal guide to all things book-writing and was my life coach when it came to navigating the process of ghost-writing a book with someone. Kelly, I don't know how you didn't give up on me a long time ago in my apathy towards racial reconciliation issues...thank you for walking along side me the whole way. I am a better person because of you. And finally, to my Savior and Rescuer, my Lord Jesus Christ, without whom I wouldn't make it through one day on this broken planet. All glory to Him who is working to make me more like Him.

Endnotes

1 Bernstein, J., Blashill, P., Blistein, J., Brackett, N., Browne, D., DeCurtis, A., Diehl, M., Dolan, J., Eddy, C., Edmonds, B., Edwards, G., Eliscu, J., Ehrlrich, B., Exposito, S., Fricke, D., Gardner, E., George-Warren, H., Greene, A., Kory Grow, K., et.al. (2020, September 22). *The 500 Greatest Albums of All Time.* Rolling Stone Magazine. Retrieved April 9, 2022, from https://www.rollingstone.com/music/music-lists/best-albums-of-all-time-1062063/marvin-gaye-whats-going-on-4-1063232/

2 Mojo Music Magazine Staff. (2021, February 9). *The Top 10 Motown Albums.* Mojo Music Magazine. Retrieved April 9, 2022, from https://www.mojo4music.com/articles/the-mojo-list/the-top-10-motown-albums/

3 Sidu river bridge. (n.d.) In *Wikipedia.* Retrieved April 9, 2022, from https://en.wikipedia.org/wiki/Sidu_River_Bridge

4 History.com Editors. November 30, 2017 (Updated September 30, 2019). *Mesopotamia.* History.com. Retrieved April 18, 2022, from https://www.history.com/topics/ancient-middle-east/mesopotamia

5 Hallman, Carly. n.d. *The Wealthiest Historical Figures and How Much They Would be Worth in Today's Dollars.*

Titlemax. Retrieved April 18, 2022, from https://www.titlemax.com/discovery-center/money-finance/wealthiest-historical-figures-in-todays-dollars/

6   Elwes, J. & Brown, A. (2014, November 13). *How Does India's Caste System Work?*. Prospect Magazine. Retrieved April 18, 2022, from https://www.prospectmagazine.co.uk/magazine/how-does-indias-caste-system-work

7   University of Minnesota College of Liberal Arts Center for Holocaust and Genocide Studies. n.d. *Rwanda*. Retrieved April 18, 2022, from https://cla.umn.edu/chgs/holocaust-genocide-education/resource-guides/rwanda

8   History.com Editors. (2019, October 30). *Bosnian Genocide* History.com. Retrieved April 18, 2022, from https://www.history.com/topics/1990s/bosnian-genocide

9   Christianity.com Editors. (n.d.) *Deuteronomy*. Christianity.com. Retrieved April 10, 2022, from https://www.christianity.com/bible/niv/deuteronomy/

10 Mintz, Steven. (n.d.) *Historical Context: Was Slavery the Engine of American Economic Growth?* The Gilder Lehrman Institute of American History. Retrieved April 18, 2022, from https://www.gilderlehrman.org/history-resources/teaching-resource/historical-context-was-slavery-engine-american-economic-growth

11 Olson, J. E. & Bourne, E. G. (1906). *The Northmen, Columbus, and Cabot*. Charles Scribner's Sons.

12 *Behind The Name*. (n.d.) Retrieved April 20, 2022, from https://www.behindthename.com/name/christopher

13 Whitfield, George. (1743). *A Letter to the Negroes lately converted to Christ in America. And particularly to those, lately called out of darkness, into God's marvellous light, at*

Mr. Jonathan Bryan's in South Carolina. Or A welcome to the believing Negroes, into the household of God. J. Hart, Printer.

14 Shipp, A. M. (1844). *The History of Methodism in South Carolina.* Southern Methodist Publishing House.

15 The White House Historical Association Staff. (n.d.) *Slavery in the President's Neighborhood FAQ.* Retrieved April 20, 2022, from https://www.whitehousehistory. org/slavery-in-the-presidents-neighborhood-faq#:~:- text=A%3A%20According%20to%20surviving% 20documentation%2C%20at%20least%20twelve%20pres- idents%20were,Andrew%20Johnson%2C%20and%20 Ulysses%20S

16 Jefferson, T. (1783). *Notes on the State of Virginia.* Prichard and Hall. Retrieved April 22, 2022, from https:// docsouth.unc.edu/southlit/jefferson/jefferson.html cour- tesy of University of North Carolina at Chapel Hill, 2006.

17 National Park Service Staff. (n.d.) *Second Debate: Freeport, Illinois.* National Park Service Lincoln Home (National Historic Site Illinois). Retrieved April 26, 2022, from https://home.nps.gov/liho/learn/historyculture / debate2.htm

18 Kerim, S. (2019, April 16) *Ring Around the Rosie – A Song for the Plague.* Medium.com. Published in Weird History. Retrieved on April 22, 2022, from https://medium.com/ weird-history/ring-around-the-rosie-a-song-for-the- plague-4647a45b01b1

19 Stewart, B. E. (2004, May 25). *Stone Mountain.* New Georgia Encyclopedia. Retrieved April 22, 2022, from https://www.georgiaencyclopedia.org/articles/ geography-environment/stone-mountain/

20 Letter from Robert E. Lee to Mary Randolph Custis Lee. December 27, 1856. Fort Brown, Texas. Retrieved April 22, 2022, from https://encyclopediavirginia.org/entries/letter-from-robert-e-lee-to-mary-randolph-custis-lee-december-27-1856/

21 Jefferson Davis' reply in the Senate to William H. Seward. February 29, 1860. Senate Chamber, U.S. Capitol. Retrieved April 22, 2022, from https://jeffersondavis.rice.edu/archives/documents/jefferson-davis-reply-senate-william-h-seward

22 Allen, Jonathan R. (n.d.) Jefferson Davis resigns from the United States Senate. Quoting Jefferson Davis' farewell speech to the United States Senate. January 21, 1861. Senate Chamber, U.S. Capitol. Retrieved April 22, 2022, from https://www.nellaware.com/blog/jefferson-davis-resigns-from-the-united-states-senate.html

23 *Emancipation Memorial.* (n.d.) National Park Service Website. Retrieved April 22, 2022, from https://www.nps.gov/places/000/emancipation-memorial.htm

24 *Emancipation Group. Public Art Update.* City of Boston Website. Retrieved April 22, 2022, from https://www.boston.gov/departments/arts-and-culture/emancipation-group

25 Natanson, H., Heim, J., Miller, M., and Jamison, P. (2020, June 26). Protestors denounce Abraham Lincoln statue in D.C., urge removal of Emancipation Memorial. *The Washington Post.* Retrieved April 22, 2022, from https://www.washingtonpost.com/local/protesters-denounce-abraham-lincoln-statue-in-dc-urge-removal-of-emancipation-memorial/2020/06/25/02646910-b704-11ea-a510-55bf26485c93_story.html

26 White, J. and Sandage, S. (2020, June 30). What Frederick Douglass had to say about monuments." *Smithsonian Magazine*. Retrieved April 22, 2022, from https://www.smithsonianmag.com/history/what-frederick-douglass-had-say-about-monuments-180975225/

27 Southern Poverty Law Center Staff. (n.d.) *Whose Heritage? Public Symbols of the Confederacy.* Southern Poverty Law Center. Retrieved April 22, 2022, from https://www.splcenter.org/20190201/whose-heritage-public-symbols-confederacy

28 NBC Sports.com Staff. (2020a, June 15). *Before becoming a Maryland legend, Len Bias was just a local kid with untapped potential.* NBC Sports. Retrieved April 26, 2022, from https://www.nbcsports.com/washington/maryland-terps/becoming-maryland-legend-len-bias-was-just-local-kid-untapped-potential

29 NBC Sports.com Staff. (2020b, June 15). *Before becoming a Maryland legend, Len Bias was just a local kid with untapped potential.* NBC Sports. Retrieved April 26, 2022, fromhttps://www.nbcsports.com/washington/maryland-terps/becoming-maryland-legend-len-bias-was-just-local-kid-untapped-potential

30 National Geographic Society. (n.d.) *The 13th Amendment to the United States Constitution.* In National Geographic Encyclopedia. Retrieved April 26, 2022, from https://www.nationalgeographic.org/encyclopedia/13th-amendment-united-states-constitution/

31 Taylor, J., & Stevenson, B. (2020a). *Reconstruction in America: Racial violence after the Civil War, 1865-1876.* Equal Justice Initiative.

32 Taylor, J., & Stevenson, B. (2020b). *Reconstruction in America: Racial violence after the Civil War, 1865-1876.* Equal Justice Initiative.

33 Vicksburg Post Staff Reports. (2020, February 17). "Wicker: Honoring the historic impact of Hiram Rhodes Revels." *The Vicksburg Post.* Retrieved April 26, 2022, from https://www.vicksburgpost.com/2020/02/17/wicker-honoring-the-historic-impact-of-hiram-rhodes-revels/

34 Taylor, J., & Stevenson, B. (2020c). *Reconstruction in America: Racial violence after the Civil War, 1865-1876.* Equal Justice Initiative.

35 U.S. Department of Housing and Urban Development Staff. (n.d.) *History of fair housing.* U.S. Department of Housing and Urban Development. Retrieved April 26, 2022, from https://www.hud.gov/program_offices/fair_housing_equal_opp/ aboutfheo/history#:~:text=On%20 April%2011%2C%201968%2C%20President,Civil%20 Rights%20Act%20of%201964

36 Du Bois, W.E.B. (1935). *Black Reconstruction: An essay toward a history of the part which black folk played in the attempt to reconstruct democracy in America, 1860 – 1880.* Harcourt, Brace and Company.

37 Jefferson, Thomas. (1783). *Notes on the State of Virginia.* Prichard and Hall. Retrieved April 22, 2022, from https://docsouth.unc.edu/southlit/jefferson /jefferson.html courtesy of University of North Carolina at Chapel Hill, 2006.

38 Berry, H. (1832). *The speech of Henry Berry, (of Jefferson), in the House of Delegates of Virginia, on the abolition of slavery.* Retrieved April 26, 2022, from https://books. google.com/books?id= kTRcAAAAcAAJ &printsec =frontcover #v=onepage&q=we%20have%20as% 20far%20as%20possible&f=false

39 National Park Service Staff. (n.d.). *Second Debate: Freeport, Illinois.* National Park Service Lincoln Home (National Historic Site Illinois). Retrieved April 26, 2022, from https://home.nps.gov/liho/learn/historyculture / debate2.htm

40 BlackPast.org. (2010, December 15). *(1866) Mississippi Black Codes.* BlackPast.org. Retrieved April 26, 2022, from https://www.blackpast.org/ african-american-history/1866-mississippi-black-codes/

41 Taylor, J., & Stevenson, B. (2020). *Reconstruction in America: Racial violence after the Civil War, 1865-1876.* Equal Justice Initiative.

42 The Jackson Sun Staff. (2001b). Examples of Jim Crow Laws – Oct. 1960 – Civil Rights. *The Jackson Sun.* Retrieved April 26, 2022, from https://www.ferris.edu/ HTMLS/news/jimcrow/links/misclink/examples.htm

43 Anderson, T. (2009, May 1). *"Ten Little Niggers": The Making of a Black Man's Consciousness.* Folklore Forum. Retrieved April 26, 2022, from https://folkloreforum. net/2009/05/01/"ten-little-niggers"-the-making-of-a-black-man's-consciousness

44 Clark, A. (2021, April 20). *How the History of Blackface is Rooted in Racism.* History.com. Retrieved April 26, 2022, from https://www.history.com/news/ blackface-history-racism-origins

45 Carroll, C. (1900). *The negro a beast…or…in the image of god.* American Book and Bible House. Scanned version available at: https://archive.org/details/

Thenegrobeastori00carrrich/page/n3/ mode/2up?ref=ol&view=theater

46 Ota Benga. (2005, January 17). In *Wikipedia*. Retrieved April 26, 2022, from https://en.wikipedia.org/wiki/Ota_Benga. For further reading, also see: Newkirk, P. (2016). *Spectacle: The Astonishing Life of Ota Benga*. amistad.

47 Li, D.K. (2020, July 31). *Bronx Zoo operator apologizes for racist display of African man in 1906*. NBC News. Retrieved April 26, 2022, from https://www.nbcnews.com/news/us-news/bronx-zoo-operator-apologizes-racist-display-african-man-1906-n1235457

48 Florio, J. and Shapiro, O. (2018, June 22). *When Joe Louis fought Schmeling, white America enthusiastically rooted for a black man*. Andscape.com. Retrieved April 26, 2022, from https://theundefeated.com/features/when-joe-louis-fought-schmeling-white-america-enthusiastically-rooted-for-a-black-man/

49 Business News Staff. October 31, 2021. *How much does discrimination hurt the economy? (Ep. 480)* [Audio podcast]. Business News.in. Transcript retrieved on April 26, 2022, from https://businessnews.in/2021/10/31/how-much-does-discrimination-hurt-the-economy-ep-480/

50 Beschloss, M. (2014, October 17). Knocked down by life, Joe Louis could rely on his friends. *The New York Times*. Retrieved on April 26, 2022, from https://www.nytimes.com/2014/10/18/upshot/knocked-down-by-life-joe-louis-could-rely-on-his-friends.html

51 Max Schmeling. (2002, November 13). In *Wikipedia*. Retrieved April 26, 2022, from https://en.wikipedia.org/wiki/Max_Schmeling

52 Miller, R. (2020, May 16). Dealing: the incredible journey of an African American car dealer. *Automotive Business*.

53 Pietila, A. (2010a). *Not in my neighborhood: how bigotry shaped a great American city.* Ivan R. Dee.

54 Pietila, A. (2010b). *Not in my neighborhood: how bigotry shaped a great American city.* Ivan R. Dee. Also see: https://www.law.cornell.edu/wex/shelley_ v_kraemer_ (1948) for the full opinion in the Shelley v. Kramer case.

55 Madrigal, A. (2014, May 22). *The racist housing policy that made your neighborhood.* The Atlantic. Retrieved April 26, 2022, from https://www.theatlantic.com/business/ archive/2014/05/the-racist-housing-policy-that-made-your-neighborhood/371439/

56 Dreier, P., Mollenkopf, J. H., & Swanstrom, T. (2014). *Place Matters: Metropolitics for the Twenty-first century.* Amsterdam University Press.

57 The whole Underwriting Manual can be found here: https://www.huduser.gov/portal/sites/default/files/pdf/ Federal-Housing-Administration-Underwriting-Manual. pdf (Source: Kimble, J. (2007). "Insuring inequality: the role of the Federal Housing Administration in the urban ghettoization of African Americans." *Law & Social Inquiry, 32,* (2), 399–434. Retrieved August 26. 2021, from www. jstor.org/stable/20108708)

58 G.L. Holland, assistant to the VA Administrator, as noted in Woods II, Louis L., "Almost "no Negro veteran…could get a loan": African Americans, the GI Bill, and the NAACP campaign against residential segregation, 1917 – 1960", *The Journal of African American History, 98*(3), Symposium: "St. Claire Drake: The Making of a Scholar-Activist" (Summer 2013), 392 -417.

59 Michals, D. (2015). *Ruby Bridges.* National Women's History Museum. Retrieved April 26, 2022, from

https://www.womenshistory.org/education-resources/
biographies/ruby-bridges

60 Pottery Barn Rule. (2004, April 22). In *Wikipedia*.
Retrieved April 26, 2022, from https://en.wikipedia.org/
wiki/Pottery_Barn_rule

61 Boos, S. (2014). Uwe Johnson. In *Speaking the Unspeakable
in Postwar Germany: Toward a Public Discourse on the
Holocaust* (pp. 114–134). Cornell University Press. Retrieved
on April 26, 2022, from http://www.jstor.org/stable/10.7591/
j.ctt1287dgh.10

62 Vigdor, N. (2021, October 6). Germany sets aside an
additional $767 million for Holocaust survivors, officials
say." *The New York Times*. Retrieved April 26, 2022, from
https://www.nytimes.com/2021/10/06/world/europe/
holocaust-settlement-germany.html

63 U.S. Census Bureau (2021). *Historical Poverty Tables:
People and Families – 1959–2020*. Retrieved on April
26, 2022, from https://www.census.gov/data/tables/
time-series/demo/income-poverty/historical-pover-
ty-people.html. See specifically Tables 2 and 3.

64 August Landmesser. (2010, September 23). In *Wikipedia*.
Retrieved April 26, 2022, from https://en.wiki-
pedia.org/w/index.php?title=August_Landmesser
&dir=prev&action=history

65 Cox, S. (2013, June 20). *August Landmesser, the story of
the man behind the crossed arms*. All That's Interesting.
com. Retrieved on April 26, 2022, from https://allthatsin-
teresting.com/august-landmesser

66 Wyatt-Brown, B. (1969). *Lewis Tappan and the Evangelical
War Against Slavery* (First Edition). Press of Case Western
Reserve University. See also: Essig, J.D. (1978). The Lord's

free man: Charles G. Finney and his abolitionism. *Civil War History 24*(1), 25-45. <u>doi:10.1353/cwh.1978.0009</u>. See also Green, R. (1993). Charles Grandison Finney: the social implications of his ministry. *The Asbury Theological Journal, 48*: (2), 5 – 26. Available at: https://place.asbury-seminary.edu/asburyjournal/vol48/iss2/2

67 Goodwin, S. (2009). *Africa in Europe: Antiquity into the age of global expansion.* Lexington Books.